RAJASTHAN

'Nirvighnam Kuru Me deva sarva karyeshu sarvada'

Oh my lord of lords Ganesha, kindly remove all obstacles,
always and forever from all my activities and endeavours

TRADITIONAL INDIAN JEWELLERY

THE GOLDEN SMILE OF INDIA

BERNADETTE VAN GELDER

ACC Art Books

Contents

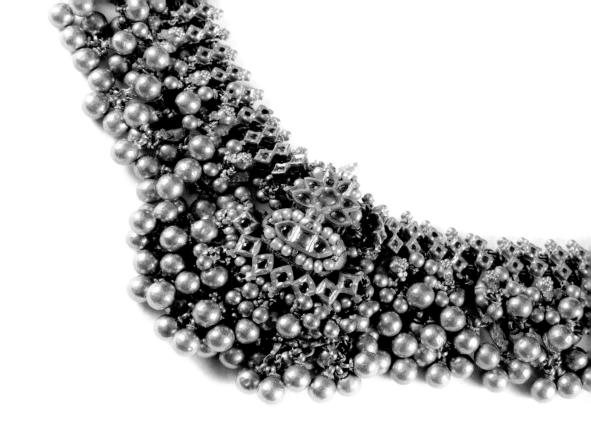

'...everything that I understand,
I understand only because I love'

Lev Tolstoy

Acknowledgements

I wish to express my gratitude to my late husband, Wim Brouwer, for his patience, for sharing his love of travelling and exploring different cultures. Our curiosity over the years has led us to spend a lot of time in India which enabled me to study the various aspects and traditions of its jewellery.

I will miss him forever.

My parents, who gave me life and planted their seeds for me to grow into the woman I have become. For giving me an awareness of beauty. They are always with me.

'As Ever' Marie Claire, Fleur and Noelle.

Special thanks to Marie Claire van Schooten-van Gelder who has shown her unstinting commitment to this project. I am indebted to her and wish to thank her for her unflagging support.

Suresh and Arun Dhaddha with their beautiful families, who have made their parents' dream come true. They were young boys when their father Gyan welcomed my husband and me into their house. I have seen them grow in so many ways and I admire how they continue their father's legacy, our bond cannot grow stronger.

Rajesh Ajmera, always at the other end of the 'line' when I was back home in the Netherlands, explaining and teaching me the 'hidden' secrets of the real thing. Together with Rajiv Arora, they became my extended family in India thirty years ago. The amazing times we often spent around the dining table with their families in their beautiful houses, which became my home away from home.

Mahipal Kothari, for his tremendous achievement and endless patience in unveiling the secret of the old enamel techniques. For his time travelling with me and making the impossible possible.

Dr Hanco Zwaan and his team at the Netherlands Gemological Laboratory Leiden, for their co-operation, for sharing their knowledge and expertise and for their enthusiastic perseverance in repeatedly clarifying complex matters to me.

All the collectors who so kindly allowed me to study and photograph many of the pieces in their collections, for this publication. A special thanks goes to:
Mr Wak Kani and his family
Rajiv Arora
Rajesh Ajmera
Simon Ray, Simon Ray Indian & Islamic Works of Art
Georgia Chrischilles
Manoj Agrawal and his family
Suresh Dhaddha and his family

Imperial Hotel in New Delhi, Rajputana Sheraton in Jaipur and the many other hotels in which we often stayed over the years during our travels in India. Thanks to all the wonderful staff who were so welcoming, and made our stays easy and pleasant, and when I started to travel on my own, they made me feel safe and secure.

Lucca, in Italy is still draped under a 'renaissance blanket', and it is at the Villa 'La Principessa' where I found the ideal soil to fill my heart and soul with almost neverending inspiration.

Thank you to the amazing staff of the Villa.

Mahaveer Swami, born in 1959, is descended from a family of traditional Bikaneri painters. As a child he began training with his father, M.R. Swami and grandfather M.D. Swami; later he studied under the late Vedpal Sharma 'Bannu' in Jaipur, Rajasthan.

Mahaveer Swami revived the best aspects of the sophisticated and refined Bikaner School of Painting, as published in this book, with an originality and brilliance unique among contemporary miniaturists.

Mahaveer Swami stands out from thousands of traditional Rajasthani painters, not only because of his great skills in drawing and painting, but also because he has the ability to recognise the difference between the truly fine and the mundane. His working style is strongly influenced by his study of Mughal and Rajasthani miniatures. His subject matter is often drawn from the life study of holy men and women, the daily life of Indian women, and sometimes from mythological themes.

Mahaveer Swami is one of the finest traditional artists working in India today, his ethereal colours and exquisite brushwork are combined with a unique inner vision and great sensitivity to the world around him. He proves that there is no real gap between *contemporary* and *traditional*, there is only *art*.

His work demonstrates beyond doubt that a rich and beautiful tradition is still very much alive.

Special thanks to Margreet Borgman and her team at Oranje Boven 'sHertogenbosch.

I would also like to express my gratitude to:
Karin and Peter Breed, goldsmiths
Mr and Mrs Ton and Marie Jose van der Vorst, for photography
Mr Renee Kuys, for photography
Mrs K. Kohlstrand, editor
Mrs B. Kat-Johnson, advisor
Mrs Mini George and Mr Rishi, Travel House Jaipur
Mr W. Greenwood, Museum of Islamic Art, Doha, Qatar

A Journey

One day, my brother Clemens van der Ven, who was a Chinese art expert, showed me a demi parure of traditional Chinese export jewellery, from the early nineteenth century. The parure consisted of a necklace, pendant, brooch, bracelet and a pair of earrings, all in the original red leather presentation box. Each piece was set in 20-carat gold and depicted flowers carved out of horn. I fell in love with its beauty. Clemens gave it to me saying that to fully appreciate this beautiful jewellery, I should study the history and culture of the country in which it was made.

That was the start of a long journey through libraries and museums, and talking with experts and scholars. I visited exhibitions and searched for the untold stories about pieces of jewellery and the famous and nameless craftspeople and artisans who created them. After reading *The Baburnama: Memoirs of Babur, Prince and Emperor*, the journey finally led me not to China but, surprisingly enough, to India.

Zahir Uddin Babur, conquered the kingdom of Delhi and laid the foundation of the Mughal empire which only ceased to exist after a mutiny in 1858; he became the first Mughal emperor (reign 1526–1530). He had a keen eye for natural beauty of every kind, and combined a fine sense of taste and style with enjoying the company of a broad spectrum of artists.

In the early eighties I began to travel to the subcontinent with my late husband. Here I learned about the religions and cultures in the different states. I met the Last Wanderers in the Thar Dessert in Rajasthan and the peoples living in the Great Rann in western Gujarat. I visited the back waters and sandy beaches of 'God's own Country', Kerala. I discovered the arts and crafts of Tamil Nadu in the south, the splendour of Hyderabad and I have witnessed holy men offering water to the sun in worship while standing in the holy river Ganges. It was fascinating to experience the centuries old temples with incredible architecture depicting gods and goddesses, to listen to the myths and legends of Hinduism, and to learn about the history of the devout Muslims in their magnificent Jama Mashids and Pearl Mosques. All of these facets of life, still so tangible and vibrant, that are apparent in every Indian person through their daily life, filled with religion, countless festivals, working the land and guiding their families. This predominantly rural society has kept its traditions vital, although there a glimpse of the twenty-first century is just perceptible. But one thing struck me time after time: the passion of the Indian people, rich or poor, for adornment in their life. Through this I came across different styles and whereabouts of traditional jewellery.

Once I started to get to grips with this subcontinent I became so overwhelmed by the different cultures, religions and languages in their multitude that I started to question my dream of building even a modest Indian jewellery collection. Could I do it justice?

Throughout my travels I was invited into traditional workshops where I witnessed the making of jewellery in all its aspects. During one of these visits, by chance I was introduced to (someone who turned out to be) a very special person. We began to talk, and I told him all about my passion for his country and its culture and that I dreamed of collecting some nice pieces of jewellery to take back with me to the Netherlands. He told us to come back the next day, which we reluctantly did.

The next day, sitting in his tiny little office, he offered us some lovely masala chai (an Indian tea) and started to unpack the most beautiful pieces of jewellery I had ever seen. My heart skipped a beat and they almost took my breath away. Was I in heaven? Was it really me, sitting and staring at these incredible marvels? This one chance encounter proved to me that I was on the right track. 'This really is me and this is what I am searching for,' I told my husband.

But at the same time I thought: 'How can I afford even one piece?' The gentleman read my mind and told me that he was impressed and moved by my reaction to the jewellery and was convinced that the two of us were meant to meet, so everything would work out for the best.

From that very moment, Gyan Chand Dhaddha from Jaipur became my teacher, guru, dearest friend and trusted source in India. He, quite literally, took me by the hand and guided me through the fascinating world of jewellery-making in India and familiarised me with the old traditional designs and techniques. He revealed to me the difference between a historical piece and the same design made today. He knew the best enamel workshops, stone-setters, artisans and designers, whether they were in Rajasthan, Delhi, Harayana, Uttar Pradesh, Madhya Pradesh, Gujarat, Bengal, Maharasthra, Tamil Nadu, Kerala or Karnataka. I followed his advice on where to go, how to look, to touch, to learn and to experience. He felt my eagerness for knowledge and explained to me that purchasing traditional jewellery is itself an art. I soon learned that India had not had a system of hallmarking, so I would need to learn to have confidence in my own knowledge, judgement, instinct and, eventually, experience.

Through his guidance and the love and patience of my dear husband, I have been able to explore and experience India (the country, the culture, the peoples and their jewellery), and to indulge my ceaseless curiosity and to learn all I can.

Gyan Chand Dhaddha, who has enriched me as an individual, died prematurely, but the magic of his spirit lives on and motivates me to this day.

My travels in India have been a constant divide between highs and lows, euphoria and tragedy, amazement and recognition, but beauty has always prevailed! It is the beauty of this country and its people, a subcontinent of such tremendous contradictions, that keeps my adrenaline going and my inspiration flowing. India itself is an experience, allow it to come in and you never know what it may mean or where it may lead you.

After years of travelling, meeting so many people (some of whom have become such dear friends that they feel like family), I wanted to share my story of how I fell in love with India, the people and their jewellery.

It is due to my dear late husband Wim Brouwer, whose wisdom, belief and endless motivation gave me 'wings' to continue, the support and encouragement that I have received from my three daughters who share with me their love for Indian jewellery, and the many people I have met in India and all over the world, that I have had the strength and the willpower to present this work.

I am well aware that mine is a Western viewpoint and that I am only lifting a corner of the veil. This work is by no means a scientific analysis and there are still many questions to be asked and much research still to be done, but it is my humble way of expressing and sharing what I know and feel about traditional Indian jewellery. I hope that you will enjoy this book and that you will be amazed and inspired by what I have been lucky enough to experience in India over the last thirty years.

Bernadette van Gelder

Gold
The Golden Smile of India

In India, references to gold have come down through an unbroken tradition from the Ramayana, Rig Veda, the Puranas and Mahabaratha

Gold is the oldest precious metal known to mankind and is universally the symbol of great treasure. Beyond being a symbol of wealth, status and purity, gold forms part of worship in Indian culture, a tradition that goes back thousands of years. Gold was the first metal to be used both for decorative purposes and personal adornment, which elevated the goldsmith's art to its highest level.

The Romans were probably the first to organise gold mining in a systematic fashion. Archaeologists have discovered evidence in Sumerian tombs at Ur in Mesopotamia of the large-scale fabrication of art objects and jewellery made from gold dating to around 3000 BC.

Gold and the Gods

In India, references to gold have come down through an unbroken tradition from the Ramayana, Rig Veda, the Puranas and Mahabaratha, but there is no record of where or when gold was mined.

Gold is associated with prosperity and the divine, specifically with Lakshmi, the goddess of wealth and good fortune. Lakshmi is one of the most popular Hindu female deities. It is likely that, because of the underlying human desire for wealth, she encompasses a large number of folk elements. Her auspicious benedictions are invoked with the giving and receiving of gold. For that reason, gold plays an important

Gold *nali*, ring
South India
Nineteenth century

Gold, repoussé-work, V-shaped ring (*nali*) depicting a *kirtimukha* with a *makara* on either side. A gold bead is attached below by gold wire.

Kirtimukha, or face of glory, is the name of a fierce-looking monster face with huge fangs and a gaping mouth. Makara is a mythical sea creature, half terrestrial and half aquatic.

role during the festival of Diwali, the festival of light, which is dedicated to the goddess Lakshmi. Men, women and children adorn themselves with dazzling jewellery and fineries on their head, around their neck, waist and hips, arms, hands and fingers, ankles and toes, particularly on the joints and pressure points, which helps to regulate the flow of *prana* (life breath), keeping the body and mind in balance.

Out of respect for its association with gods and goddesses, gold is never worn below the hip or touched by the leg or foot except by those of royal birth and a few others to whom permission is favourably granted. An exception is the Ursu community in Karnataka and Rajput, who wear gold anklets and toe rings. Why this fascination for gold? Its origin lies in ancient times and the Rig Veda says: 'men who donate gold shall receive a light and glorious life.' In Sanskrit, gold is called *hiranya;* the *Hiranyagarbha* (Golden Womb) is the source of all life and creation, and is manifested in the form of Brahma, the Hindu god of creation. It is believed that Brahma was born from the *Hiranyagarbha* in the form of a lotus that emerged from the navel of the god Vishnu as he reclined on the primordial ocean.

The vital chakra of the heart is depicted as a golden-yellow colour in Ayurveda, and is associated with the warmth and brightness of the sun, the giver of life. In early sacred texts, gold is seen as operating in synergy with magic and the power of a gold talisman could magically be transferred to the wearer through physical contact.[1]

Because pure gold does not corrode or rust, Hindus assign gold an immortal status, a representative of light and the inextinguishable continuity of life. In some areas, the primary ornament denoting marriage is made of gold, because it is considered to be ritually pure and sacred to the gods.

Offerings in gold are made to the temples by devotees when their special prayers are answered. Up to US$1 trillion in gold was held by temples in India, according to the *National Post* 24 April 2015: 'In 2011, a supreme court team discovered $ 22 billion worth of gold in the 16th century Sree Padmanabhaswamy Temple in the capital of Kerala State, Thiruvananthapuram. Much of the gold had been deposited by the local royal family. A popular belief that the gold lay wrapped with dozens of venomous snakes underground kept robbers away. The image of a snake engraved on the wall fueled the popular lore.'

Today, most jewels decorating images of gods and goddesses are fabricated from gold-coloured metal and set with coloured glass stones. The word gold is derived from the old English word 'geolo' meaning yellow. Its chemical symbol Au is derived from the Latin word *aurum*, meaning 'glowing'. Gold has a characteristic metallic yellow colour that changes when alloyed with other metals.

The western Malabar Coast and the Coromandel Coast in the east were once used extensively for exporting spices and other commodities, as verified by the discovery of immense quantities of Roman, Greek, Chinese and Arabian gold and silver coins during archaeological excavations in India. Gold was also acquired through conquest and trade taxes. This system remained unchanged for centuries; that is how India came to be in possession of more gold than it had deposits.

Goldsmith weighing gold

Through the ages, acquiring gold and gold jewellery has been important for the people of India. The love of jewellery was universal but it also had a special status as a medium of exchange. There is no possession more valuable, it provides financial security and its intrinsic value makes it a very good investment. People wear their gold jewellery with pride and almost all of it at the same time, since it reflects their social status and wealth. Hendley refers to the famous missionary, the Abbey Jean-Antoine Dubois (1765–1848) who authored the book *Hindu Manners, Customs and Ceremonies*: 'it is common belief among Hindus that there must always be at least a speck of gold on one's person, in order to ensure personal ceremonial purity.'[2]

The value of gold is determined by purity and weight, which is reported daily in Indian newspapers and the gold prices are quoted per gramme. For ready-to-wear items the market may evaluate pieces differently, but again it always starts with the weight and the purity. The price of gold also increases towards the marriage season with the demand for dowry jewellery. There is a clear difference between the rate applied to solid objects and that for hollow pieces.

The valuation of early jewellery demands a different approach because it deals with unique pieces. The work involved here might also contain precious stones and pearls. If such an early piece shows enamel work, then what is the condition of the enamel, and how rare is the piece? Early gold or silver jewellery may have been stored for generations and worn only once, so could appear to be pristine, even recently made. All of these factors can influence the value of a jewel.

In India, the preference is for 20/22 karat gold (90% gold and 10% alloys, silver, copper and platinum) when making jewellery. If it is too pure then the gold becomes too soft for ordinary use and it needs to be hardened by alloying with different metals.

A typical Indian technique for fabricating 20/22 karat gold jewellery (very soft) is to fill the piece with wax resin to prevent the gold from being damaged in production. There are two kinds of wax used in gold ornaments: *pachra* is reddish-brown in colour and light in weight; *surma* is a lead wax, blackish in colour and heavier in weight. If a gold piece has the support of *pachra* wax then the gold content will be higher in proportion to its total weight.

Sourcing

Gold is scarce and always in great demand. With only a few of its gold mines working—Kolar Gold Fields of Mysore (Karnataka, the most active) and the Hutti Gold Field in Hyderabad (Andhra Pradesh)—and producing about 0.5% of the country's annual gold consumption, India is a minor producer. To satisfy the local appetite, its dependence on imports of gold has increased over time, up to almost 1,000 tons each year.[3] Because of the traditional preference of Indians for storing gold in the form of jewellery, the custom grew for succeeding generations to recycle precious metals and so it became a second important source. The gold was melted down and reworked by skilful goldsmiths, almost without any loss of material. This is the main reason why it is rare to come across early pieces of jewellery and early gold artifacts. The system of hallmarks did not exist in ancient times, so jewellers tested gold on a *kasuti* (black touchstone) to be assured of the purity of the gold before accepting it to be recycled. Since the early 1990s India has been recycling approximately 92 tons of gold each year and it expects to meet around thirty per cent of its yearly demand.

In India today, gold is sourced from Switzerland, Dubai and London through:

1. A government-designated agency called MMTC (Minerals and Metal Trading Corporation);
2. Banks that have been authorised by the government to import gold to sell on the open market. The Gold Control Act of 1963 made it illegal for any individual to own more than two kilogrammes of gold;
3. Exporters that are allowed to import directly for their export orders. They are not allowed to sell the gold within the country.

Mining in India stopped some time ago due to high cost constraints but its reintroduction is being considered and new areas are being researched with the help of new technology.

In a certain area of Bikaner I have seen men and women sweeping the pavements and searching in the gullies near goldsmiths' workshops hoping to find tiny pieces of gold that may have been overlooked. They may even pay the goldsmith a small fee to collect the gold dust which has remained on the touchstone, floor or their furniture in the workshop. This practice has existed for centuries in India, although in a different way as we learn from the famous French gem merchant and traveller in the seventeenth century, Jean Baptiste Tavernier. In his *Travels in India*, Tavernier mentions; 'far from allowing so small a thing to be lost, they collect it with the aid of a ball, made half of black pitch and half of wax, with which they rub the stone which carries the gold, and at the end of some years they burn the ball and so obtain the gold which it has accumulated.' He goes on to explain; 'This trade of collecting the sweepings of goldsmith's shops is carried out by workmen known as Niyariya, separators.'[4]

Ladies searching in the gullies for pieces of gold. Jaisalmer

'The Sonis, or goldsmiths, sell their shop clearings, and even the right to break up their shop floors, to dust-washers or Demldhoyas. I was shown a large house in the city of Jaipur, which was built out of such washings.'[5]

Although being a *soni*, or goldsmith, is a predominantly male occupation, there is a notable exception in the state of Karnataka where women work to help out their family members, but they will never start their own workshop. The Indian goldsmith is known as *soni or sonar* in North India, although the name might differ in other parts of the subcontinent.

Gold and Marriage

It is almost a religious duty to provide a wife with gold jewellery if one can afford it. It plays an important part in bridal jewellery all over the subcontinent, although design and style vary between areas. The quantity and value of the jewellery is determined by the wealth of the family, but even poor families go deep into debt trying to provide some gold for their daughters. Giving gold at the time of marriage is not purely an economic transaction, but also protects the future wife from possible difficulties and hardships.

Gold is the preferred precious metal for urban and wealthy people and thus these women would never wear silver ornaments, afraid of being considered rural or of a lower class. Almost every upper-class Hindu family has its own goldsmith, to whom it gives its orders. The custom used to be for the employer to oversee the gold being melted and even for the ornament to be made in his presence, or under the watchful eye of a member of his family. Today there are many modern jewellery shops, large and small, splendidly fitted out with up-to-date displays and a large staff to assist consumers.

Most of the purchasing of gold jewellery happens during the winter marriage season (September–March) by groups of family members including brides-to-be. In India the famous festivals *Akshay Tritiya,* which is a highly auspicious and holy day for Hindus and Jains, and *Dhanteras,* the first day of Indian *Diwali,* are especially popular for buying gold jewellery.

1. Gonda, 'The functions and significance of gold in the Veda', pp.103–105.
2. Hendley, *Indian Jewellery*, p.102.
3. The *Times of India*, 20 November 2011.
4. Tavernier, *Travels in India*, Vol.1, p.35.
5. Hendley, *Indian Jewellery*, Vol.1, part V, p.81.

Gold image of Lord Ganesha
Tamil Nadu, Mahabalipuram or Chennai
Early twentieth century

height: 11 cm
width: 7 cm

Gold image of Lord Ganesha in a *swami* relief representation, in his fourteenth manifestation as Vijaya Ganapati (Giver of Success). He wears a crown set with rose-cut diamonds and featuring a large rose-cut diamond in the centre. His third eye is set in the centre of his forehead, and he sits on a throne-like seat, his four arms representing the four *antahakarana*, the inner equipment of man, the mind, the intellect, the conditioned consciousness and the ego.

In his upper left hand he holds a *paasha* (noose) and in his upper right hand he holds an *ankusha* (elephant goad). In his lower left hand he holds one of his favourite fruits, a pomegranate; in his lower right hand he holds his broken tusk. His trunk is turned to the left and he wears several long garlands around his neck. Around his large belly he carries a *naga* (snake) as a girdle or belt. He is in a seated position, his left leg folded and his right leg hanging down. Around both legs and feet he wears *payal* (anklets). Below his left foot rests his *vahana* (vehicle or mount) the mouse/rat, that represents the subjugated demon of vanity and impertinence.

Swami Jewellery
Repoussé gold or silver work in Swami-style jewellery and works of art, is an Anglo–Indian fusion style that flourished during the peak period of the British Raj (1858–1947) in India. The ornamentation often consisted of figures of the Puranic gods in high relief. The characteristic Swami-style jewellery was manufactured mainly for the Western market.

The company of P. Orr & Sons in the Madras Presidency, now Chennai, Tamil Nadu created this type of technique in ca. 1849 and it was popular until the early twentieth century. The gold ornaments were available in 22 karat gold at P. Orr & Sons and stamped as such, ORR 22, which was remarkable because no system of hallmarking was practised in India.

The jewellery of South India is unique and techniques of manufacture are distinct to the region. Repoussé, or nakashu-velai, is a technique where first the outline of the design is drawn on a sheet of gold and is then beaten from the back until the design comes out. In this piece, the reverse is covered with a plain gold plate and etched with a floral design.

Ganesha
In the Hindu pantheon this elephant-headed creature, endowed with a gentle and affectionate nature, is the God of Wisdom, the patron of science, arts and all creative activities. He is the presiding deity of material riches and also the lord of spirituality. He is seen as the remover of obstacles and is one of the most widely worshipped deities in India, regarded by millions with love and adoration. Simple everyday routines, a new business, a journey, even an examination, are all preceded by a prayer to Lord Ganesha, beseeching his benediction. He is propitiated before the start of any ceremony or ritual and is also invoked as the Lord of Letters before the start of writing sessions. He is present in almost every family shrine, where he is usually placed to the south, the direction of the demons, to defend the other gods from their baneful influences. Ganesha exists in thirty-two forms or manifestations; each form befits one of the various roles undertaken by him. Ganesha's multifaceted persona also descends to mankind through a multitude of myths and, according to the Puranas (Hindu scriptures and epics), he is the son of Lord Shiva and his consort Paravati. Why a human body with an elephant head? Of the many explanations the most popular is probably how Paravati invited the nine grahas (nine celestial Hindu deities) to see this beautiful child, among them Shani (Saturn) who would not look up at the baby and had his neck bent as a result. Then Paravati asked Shani why he was reluctant to look at her son and he answered that there was a curse laid on him by his jealous wife, under which anyone he looked at with admiration would be destroyed. Paravati insisted that Shani should look at her son and immediately Ganesha's head got separated from his body and flew off into space. Paravati wailed and lamented so loudly that Vishnu, seeing what had happened, started to search immediately for a head to replace the lost one. He found a herd of sleeping elephants and chose one of them, took his head, and placed it on the child's neck, before breathing life into the boy and taking him to his mother. Paravati was overjoyed to have a son with the wisdom and power of an elephant.

Gold *vanki*, *bazuband*, with *nali*, gold ring
Tamil Nadu, Pondichery, 1883

Red leather casket with red velvet lining that holds a set of elaborate, rigid, gold jewellery: an upper arm V-shaped ornament known as a *vanki* or *keyuram*, and a V-shaped ring called a *nali*.

The gold *vanki* is worked in repoussé from sheet gold, and bears a detailed relief of Krishna in a dancing posture, playing the flute and leaning against a bull that is licking his front foot. On either side of Krishna is an *apsara* (celestial figure in flight), each of which is flanked by a bird and two mythical winged creatures, with two elephants below. Above Krishna is a *kirtimukha* (face of glory) motif flanked by parrots. The *vanki* is set with one cabochon ruby 'holding' a ring with a bunch of pearls. A single pearl is seen on top of Krishna's head and another at the top of the armlet.

On the reverse, the *vanki* shows a *kirtimukha* (face of glory) surrounded by a rich floral and garland design.

The *nali*, also crafted entirely from sheet gold, depicts the goddess Lakshmi with two arms, wearing a large crown and sitting with folded legs. The goddess is flanked by two *apsaras* (celestial figures in flight). The top of the ring is decorated with a pearl, and in the centre, below, a bunch of pearls is suspended beneath a cabochon ruby.

This kind of repoussé workmanship is characteristic of South India. The sheet gold is worked from behind and the design is raised in high relief to the front, filled with resin (lac) to support the thin gold, and a plain gold sheet covers the back.

The V-shaped armlet consists of two parts hinged together and can be opened by unscrewing both parts. It is worn on the upper arm, above the elbow. This form of armlet is unique to South India and still popular today. It was believed that wearing a vanki *would help relieve pain during labour.*

Further information:
Stronge, *The Jewels of India*, p.121,
Jewels that Enchanted the World, p.92, illustration 35, and p.93, illustration 36
Bala Krishnan and Kumar, *Dance of the Peacock*, p.93, illustration 128, and p.187, illustration 300

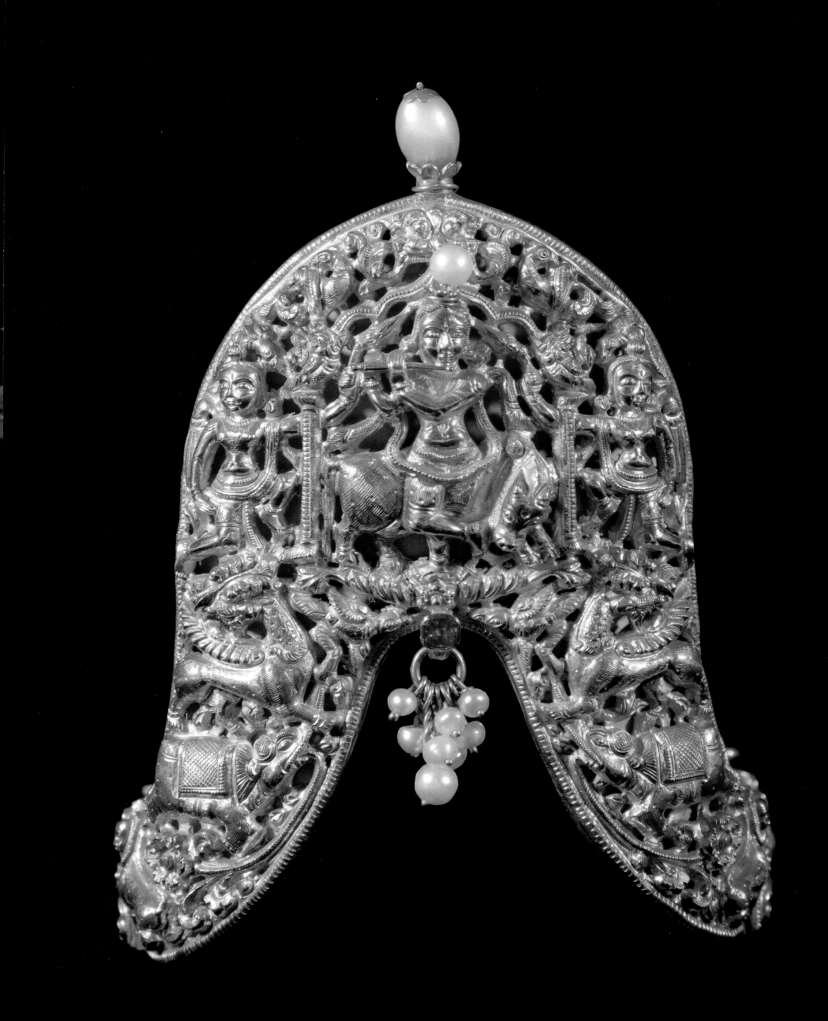

Gold *tagri*, belt
South India
Nineteenth century

length: 84 cm
weight: 315 g

Gold belt consisting of ninety-four circular plaques depicting the three most important characters from the great Hindu epic Ramayana.

In the centre is Rama, also known as Maryada Pursottam (the perfect man). On his left is his step-brother Lakshmana and on his right, his wife Sita. In his left hand Rama carries a giant *dhanush* (bow), which only he can lift, string and even break in two, according to legend. On his back he carries a quiver with four *teer* (arrows). Lakshmana carries a smaller bow on his left shoulder and a quiver with four arrows on his back. All three wear large crowns and are adorned with jewelled fineries. Rama and Lakshmana wear *dhotis* draped from their waists; Sita wears a sari.

Rama as the seventh incarnation of Lord Vishnu is the most popular symbol of chivalry and virtue. He is the embodiment of truth and morality, the ideal son, the ideal husband and above all, the ideal king. He is seen as an archetype of righteousness and the most sought-after virtues in life. Unstitched clothing is a mark of high status and is considered pure among Hindus.

The three main characters from the ancient Hindu epic Ramayana in the Shantinath Mandir at Bamotar Village near Pratapgarh, Rajasthan. Rama is in the middle with Sita to his right and to his left his step-brother Lakshmana. Hanuman, who participated in Rama's war so he could rescue Sita from the demon king Ravana, is kneeling and with folded hands, at Sita's side. Hanuman represents devotion, power, humanity and discipline.

Pandadi, two pairs of gold ear pendants
Gujarat, Saurashtra and Kutch
Early twentieth century

diameter: 6 cm
weight: 45 g each

Traditional gold *pandadi* worn in the helix by women of the
Harijan and Rabari community in Kutch.

Further information:
Ganguly, *Earrings, Ornamental Identity and Beauty in India*, p.83
Weihreter, *Schatze der Menschen und Gotter*, p.78, illustration 59

Gold *mudichu,* ear ornaments
Tamil Nadu, Southern District

Pair of gold *mudichu,* symbolising eternity in the form of an endless knot. A screw ending in a large golden ball connects both sides of the hinge; the ball functions as a decorative element.

In Nagercoil, close to the tip of the Indian peninsula, in the most southern Indian state of Tamil Nadu, are around thirty artisans who braid the thin gold wire used in this type of ear ornament.

Further information:
Ganguly, *Earrings, Ornamental Identity and Beauty in India,* p.237
Bala Krishnan, *Dance of the Peacock,* p.172, illustration 259
Untracht, *Traditional Jewelry of India,* p.220, illustration 438

Gold *visirimurugu,* ear ornaments
Tamil Nadu, Vellore District
Late nineteenth/early twentieth century

Gold repoussé fan-shaped ear pendants depicting a *kirtimukha*
(face of glory), flanked by floral ornaments. Round the lower
edge are thirteen small rings each ornamented with a flower and
a gold hollow ball (*ghunghru*).

This type of ear ornament is worn in the outer rim of the auricle.

Further information:
Hendley, *Indian Jewellery*, plate 97, illustration 658
Ganguly, *Earrings, Ornamental Identity and Beauty in India*, p.245
Aitken, *When Gold Blossoms*, p.14, figure 9

Gold *kolhapuri saj*, marriage necklace
South India and Maharashtra
Late nineteenth century

Elaborate marriage necklace (*kolhapuri saj*) consisting of three gold chains, each decorated with small grooved gold beads, comprising a series of eighty-five gold pendants, stamped, chased and filled with *lac*. The three rows are attached on either side to a gold triangle-shaped ornament depicting a *kirtimukha* (face of glory) worked in high relief with fine detailing. Eighty-two pendants have decorative, mythological and religious symbolic value and are auspicious emblems for a happy married life. Various pendants represent the symbols of the ten incarnations of Lord Vishnu and other *Vaishnavite* symbols such as: cobra, fish, conch, double eagle, *kirtimukha* and tiger claw; each row has a central marriage ornament (*thali*).

In this necklace there are fourteen distinct decorative and symbolic designs:

1. *container-shaped symbol for holding sacred verses to induce well-being;*
2. *native fruit;*
3. *representation of the summit of a temple;*
4. *two swans—symbol of the Mysore Dynasty;*
5. *crescent moon;*
6. *kirtimukha mask;*
7. *snake hood, which adorns Lord Vishnu;*
8. *conch shell;*
9. *tortoise;*
10. *flower bud;*
11. *fish;*
12. *champa (jasmine) bud;*
13. *various decorative motifs;*
14. *various flower motifs.*

It is predominantly a Vaishnavite necklace, worn by women who are devout followers of Lord Vishnu, the creator of the universe and preserver.

Both triangle-shaped finials of the necklace bear a kirtimukha mask (face of glory, sometimes also known as a lion face or demon face) flanked by floral creepers and a gold decoration. The word mukha in Sanskrit means 'face', kirti means 'fame' or 'glory'. Kirtimukha is seen by Hindus as symbolic of the glory of divine power. The kirtimukha is an architectural and decorative motif, especially in South Indian architecture, placed above entrances to Shiva temples, archways, gates, etc. as a form of protection. The monstrous face has bulging eyeballs, thick eyebrows (a suggestion of stout horns) and a gaping maw with prominent fangs or canine teeth.

In different places, kirtimukha is given different names, and different legends are spread around it, but Shaiva texts explain the origin of kirtimukha. The legend recounts that Shiva was to marry Paravati, but the king of the demons also planned to marry her. When a messenger, sent by the demon king, told Shiva about his king's plan, he became so angry that he created a monster in the shape of a man-lion and ordered the monster to eat the unfortunate messenger. However, the messenger begged Shiva to spare him, since he was only the messenger of this bad news, and Shiva sent him back. The monster complained to Shiva about his hunger, and Shiva advised him that he should eat himself, which the monster promptly did. He started with his tail, proceeding to his arms and finally his body until only his face remained. Shiva was so pleased with the result that he gave it the name 'face of glory'. Kirtimukha represents all-consuming greed.

Gold pendant
South India
Early twentieth century

This gold repoussé head ornament, adapted to be a pendant, is backed with two inscribed silver plates. The interior is filled with *lac*. The object depicts the goddess Lakshmi, smiling and standing under the protection of a five-headed cobra, her two upper arms holding a blooming lotus flower in each hand and her two lower hands are shown in a boon-giving gesture. The goddess is elegantly crowned, and wears large earrings, bangles on her four arms and a jewelled belt. There is a garland decoration on either side. Twenty-three gold discs soldered to eleven gold balls are attached to the centrepiece.

Gold *toda*, necklace
Uttar Pradesh
Late nineteenth century

Long gold necklace (*toda*) consisting of five
rows of faceted gold beads connected by
gold wire. The five gold rows are attached to
gold finials of triangular shape and set with
turquoise in a floral design.

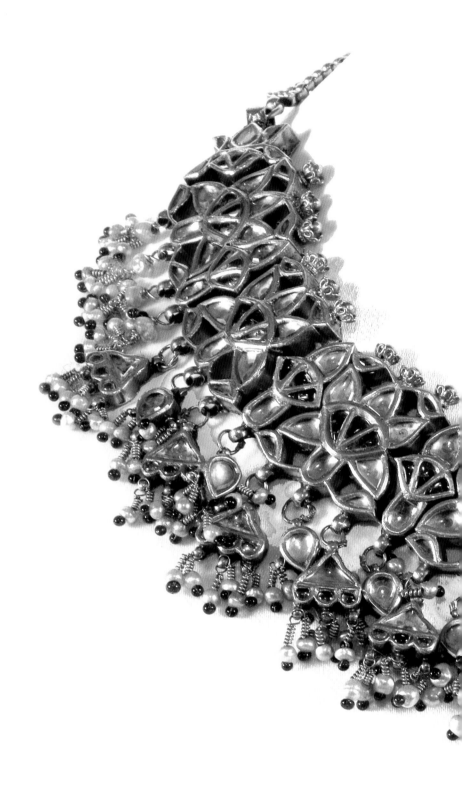

Gold necklace
Uttar Pradesh
Nineteenth century

A necklace consisting of finely worked units, alternating in design between openworked flowering lotuses and flower buds, all *kundan*-set with foiled white sapphires and emeralds. Suspended beneath are triangular and *beetal*-shaped pendants with fringes of pearls and green glass beads.

Gold head decoration
North India
Late nineteenth century

diameter: 6 cm
weight: 15 g

Elaborate gold jewel worn by women on the left side of the head.
The design shows a *makara* on either side and in the centre a pot
with a flowering tree of life symbol. The two birds on top and the
two below are surrounded by flowers. The jewel is bordered with
small circular gold discs, connected by gold wire to a second row
that encircles half the jewel from which are suspended irregular
pearls with tiny blue glass beads as finials. The girl in the painting
to the left is wearing a very similar head decoration.

A Nautch Girl with a Hookah painted by Mortimer Menpes
(1855–1939), an Australian artist who travelled in 1880 and
1890 through Japan, India, Burma, Morocco, Cairo, Mexico and
Venice. The artworks he made on these travels were exhibited in
London on his return there.

Further information:
Spink, *A Journey Through India: pictures of India by British artists*

A Nautch Girl with a Hookah: Image courtesy of Spink & Son, London,
and also Simon Ray, London

Gold *choti,* hair ornament
North India
Early nineteenth century

weight: 72 g

Gold *choti,* attached to two single loop-in-loop gold chains, consisting of a large dome-shaped openworked top part with gold beads and bells. The lower part has six smaller openworked dome-shaped ornaments with gold beads and bells hanging from the upper part. All the domes show a flower-and-leaf design.

Different designs of choti are worn as decorative finials at the end of long braided hair in rural and urban India.

Gold *jadanaagam,* hair ornament
South India, Tamil Nadu
Late nineteenth century

An elaborate gold braid ornament composed of thirteen flat plates, strung together on three black cotton threads, edged with little gold balls and decorated on either side with a mythical lion. The top of the ornament shows the five-headed divine cobra, Anantha, whose intertwined coils fall to just above a pair of mythical lions. The hood of the cobra surmounts Krishna who sits on a cow while playing his flute. On the second plate is Lord Vishnu in a relaxed pose with his consort Lakshmi, who is shown caressing his feet. A lotus-like throne accommodates Vishnu, sitting on Shesha (Anantha) the mythical serpent. Towards the left Lord Brahma arises on a lotus from Vishnu's belly button. On the right side of Lord Vishnu stands Garuda with his hands folded and Hanuman sits beneath. The plate below depicts an *apsara* (celestial figure) on either side. The lower part, above the tassel, shows a peacock on both sides and two mythical lions. A gold dome-shaped *choti* (tassel) with black silk threads, is attached beneath as a finial.

The name of the coiled snake king Sehsha/Anantha means 'eternity'. He is the naga raja *or king of all nagas and one of the primal beings of creation. He is associated with Lord Vishnu and seen as a huge serpent with between five and a thousand heads or hoods, overhanging one or more deities. In the Puranas, Shesha is said to hold all the planets of the universe on his hoods. He is considered to be a servant as well as a manifestation of Vishnu.*

Lord Shiva has different serpents that twine around his neck and hold together his matted hair, sometimes he is shown wearing earrings, belt and sacred thread in the form of serpents. The cobra is the most frequently mentioned character in Hindu mythology and is specifically related to Lord Shiva.

The gold serpent hair decoration is fixed on the triple braid and is part of the bridal jewellery in Tamil Nadu, Southern Karnataka and Andhra Pradesh. Snake-related symbols often appear in jewellery, and are worn by all classes of people all over the subcontinent.

Further information:
Bala Krishnan and Kumar, *Dance of the Peacock*, p.97, illustration 137
Untracht, *Traditional Jewelry of India*, p.51, illustration 71

Overleaf
Illustration of how a *jadanaagam* is worn

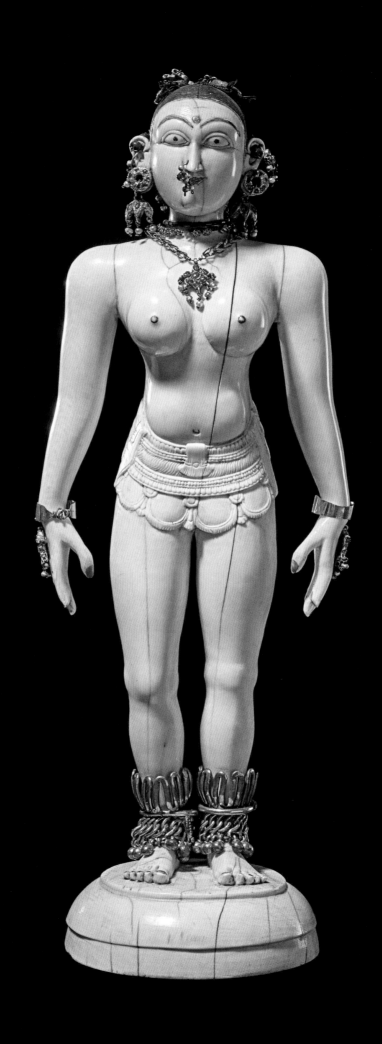

44

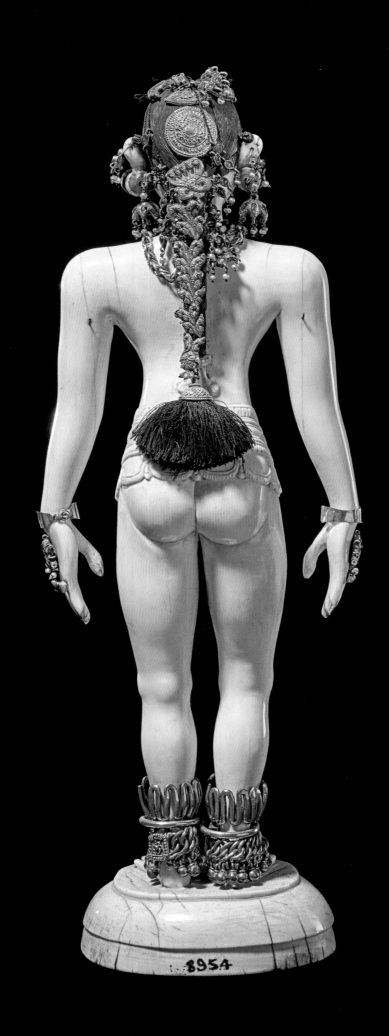

Gold *kasu malai,* necklace with gold coins
West Bengal, Murshidabad
Coins, eighteenth century
Chain and round gold spacers, twentieth century

weight: 165 g

Chain with nine identical gold coins, each with two soldered
loops, inscribed in Arabic script with the year AH 19 in the Islamic
calendar (AD 1779 Gregorian calendar). The coin 'pendants' are
alternated with ten beads each fabricated from sixteen gold
wires, soldered by a single gold wire.

*The writing on the coins 'regnal year 19' relates to the reign of Emperor
Jalaluddin Abul-Muzaffar Muhammad Ali Gauhar Shah Alam II (1728–1806)
(reign 1760–1806).*

*The use of coins in jewellery is mentioned in the Mahabharata (one of
the two epic Sanskrit poems of ancient India). In the eighteenth century,
Murshidabad was in its heyday as a centre of Mughal culture. Coins with
Arabic, Urdu and Persian inscriptions were used by independent Indian
principalities, which had their own coinage.*

*It became fashionable in the eighteenth century to have coins and pseudo
coins made into necklaces. The same applied to gold coins stamped with
the images of gods and goddesses. It symbolises value, savings, and certainly
contributes to the wearer's wealth.*

Gold *kasu malai*, coin necklace
Tamil Nadu Chennai (Madras) 1910

length: 35 cm
weight: 137 g

Gold *kasu malai*, consisting of thirty-two coins, embellished with floral-shaped tops, joined together with double loop-in-loop gold wire.

Each coin is inscribed on one side in the centre with '22 ct India 1910' and flanked by two lotus branches with a number '5' in the centre at the top. 'Sakarachan' is inscribed on the left, and 'Alakchand' on the right.

The reverse side depicts a four-armed Goddess Lakshmi, sitting on a lotus-shaped throne, with legs folded. Lakshmi wears a crown and holds a lotus flower in both her upper hands, her two lower hands are in the boon-giving and blessing gesture. Round the image of the goddess is inscribed 'Gold Maha Lackshmi Madras'.

Lakshmi is the Hindu goddess of wealth, purity, generosity and the embodiment of beauty.

Since gold coins are a symbol of wealth they may constitute a form of savings as well as enhancing the status of the wearer. Gold and silver coin necklaces are seen in different parts of the subcontinent.

Further information:
Untracht, *Traditional Jewelry of India*, p.123, illustration 207
Bala Krishnan and Kumar, *Dance of the Peacock*, p.18

Gold *putali,* floral necklace
South India, Kerala
Early twentieth century

Light, sheet gold necklace of identical oblong-shaped, floral-stamped units, fringed below with a double row of tiny pendants, each with tassels and triangle-shaped finials on either side.

Gold necklace
Kerala
First quarter twentieth century

Light sheet-gold necklace with triangular finials and identical stamped units with tassels, decorated with floral motifs and a centre decoration set with *kempukal*.

Kempukal is a red mineral, found in the riverbeds of the Manjara and Kempukal rivers in southern India, Kerala and Maharasthra. The stone is often used in temple jewellery.

Ananthamudichu, gold ear pendants
South India, Tamil Nadu
Late nineteenth century

Four-faceted ear pendants, fashioned from thin sheet gold and decorated with four leaves suspended from gold spherical finials on each of four sides. The upper part shows a sculpture design which reflects the temple architecture in Tamil Nadu. The decorated and tapering lower part also has a gold spherical finial at the tip.

Further information:
Untracht, *Traditional Jewelry of India*, p.225, illustration 461

Gold *vedhla,* earrings
Gujarat, Jamnagar district

This style of *vedhla* with spiralled wire ending in an octagonal cube was often made by Bhopa Rabari, who migrated from Rajasthan via Katchch to Jamnagar in western Gujarat. *Vedhla,* also in heavy silver, are worn in the extended lobe, often in conjunction with other earrings in the upper ear perimeter

The Bhopa Rabari women are intelligent, strong and quite tall. They are easily distinguished by their long black headscarves, which fall loosely to the ground. They are skilled in the traditional art of cloth embroidery. Their men folk, in Gujarat, prefer white garments and white turbans.

Further information:
Untracht, *Traditional Jewelry of India,* p.220, illustration 436

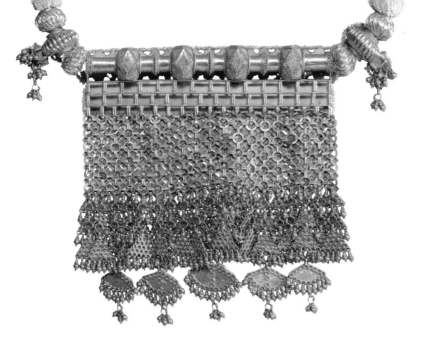

Gold *tevta,* wedding necklace
North India, Bikaner
Nineteenth century

height: 14 cm
width, upper part: 20 cm
width *jhaler,* lower part: 14.5 cm
weight: 650 g

Gold *tevta,* elaborate traditional wedding necklace worn by brides.
The rigid upper part is set with *billore* (rock crystal) on foil. On
either side is a roundel with a square pendant. The lower flexible
part (*jhaler*) is decorated with a flower in the centre and a bird
on either side; all three are set with *billore* on foil, the bodies of
the birds are blue glass. Five pendants (*tansukh*) set with *billore*
on foil are suspended from the flexible *jhaler.* All decorations
are bordered with tiny seed pearls. The *tevta* is supported with
multiple strands of white *chid* (glass seed beads), adorned with a
large gold rosette set with *billore* on foil.

The top part of the reverse shows a rigid tubular element
alternated with four large hollow beads decorated with a
granulation pattern.

A gold *jhaler* composed of interlocking rings, supports the gold
network of small square gold plaques at the front. Triangle-shaped
pendants and five oval-shaped pendants (*tansukh*) are attached to
the lower part.

*Rajasthan has long been the land of royalty, grandeur and heritage. The people
are traditional at heart and swear by their culture and rituals, especially when
it comes to weddings. There are many different forms of wedding jewellery, but
tevta is an auspicious jewel. Timaniyaan is a smaller version. These gorgeous
ornaments are worn in Bikaner, Jaisalmer, Jodhpur, Ajmer and Nagaur, the former
princely states in Rajasthan, and belong to the traditional bridal trousseau.*

Further information:
Babur's Heritage

Flexible gold *marathi* or *sankla,* bracelets
Rajasthan, Gujarat and northern Maharashtra,
Nineteenth century

outer diameter: 8.3 cm
weight, pair: 156 g

Above
A pair of flexible gold bracelets, comprising a series of forty
ingeniously entwined links, each decorated with a *kundan*-set flat-
cut diamond. An anti-clockwise screw clasp set with a diamond
inserts into hinges fitted on both ends of the bracelet.

Opposite
A similar pair with each link slightly hammered.

*Flexible chains were also worn as anklets. If made from gold they indicate that
the wearer is a privileged person, silver anklets are worn by the rural class.
A single anklet* dastband almas *in gold was awarded by a ruler as princely
recognition in a custom known as* ta'zim, *and was worn on the right ankle.*

Further information:
Untracht, *Traditional Jewelry of India*, p.275, photo 657
Jaffer, *Beyond Extravagance*, p.178
Aitken, *When Gold Blossoms*, p.120 illustration 127 (silver)
For ta'zim anklets, see: Bala Krishnan and Kumar, *Dance of the Peacock*,
p.205, photo 336

Pair of large ear ornaments
Kerala
Late nineteenth century

length: 8.3 cm
weight, pair: 105 g

Pair of elaborate large gold ear ornaments *andi bhaden kathila*,
traditionally worn by *Malayalam* Muslim women in Cochin and
Trissur district.

The ear ornaments consist of four thin gold sheets soldered
together over a *lac* core and decorated after a traditional theme
with very fine filigree work and bordered with tiny gold beads.
The ornaments are fasten with a two-hinged movable loop and a
tiny screw.

*Kathila are made by Hindu artisans and worn by Muslim women only since
the late nineteenth century also in combination with other gold earrings.*

Further information:
Van Cutsem, *A World of Earrings*, p.120
Untracht, *Traditional Jewelry of India*, p.225, illustration 460

Pahunchi, gold bracelet
North India

Traditional gold *pahunchi* consisting of gold balls filled with *lac* and with rosette finials on either side. They are strung together on black cotton in five parallel strands. The bracelet is backed and fastened with black fabric *zari* work, ending in a loop and ball.

This type of bracelet was traditional in Rajasthan and is also found in silver.

Further information:
Bhandari, *Costume, Textiles and Jewellery of India*, p.147, illustration 258

Gold choker
Madhya Pradesh, Reva District
Late nineteenth/early twentieth century

Gold necklace (choker) of loose elements bound by two gold
chains and filled in with six-faceted spheroids soldered together.
On top of each bar are three loops each with a faceted disc,
which in turn each have two smaller discs. Gold loops are
soldered to the lower side, holding gold wired rings, each carrying
patti-shaped pendants which again have wired rings with three
gold balls each as finials. The *patti* are connected by side loops
embellished with a gold ball.

Gold collar
Gujarat, Kachchh
Late nineteenth century

Gold collar consisting of very fine gold loop-in-loop wires
supported by a band of dark red cotton cloth on the inside. The
gold wires are held together by fifteen flat gold bands decorated
with roundels and flower-shaped ornaments set with foiled
coloured glass. The diamond-shaped ornament in the centre
has granulation work and white, green, red and black enamel, as
well as an oblong blue-enamelled plaque in the centre inscribed
with the name *Kumarpala* in Gujarati. Suspended below is an
openworked gold pendant set with green and red glass. The back
part is fabricated from two hollow gold tubes, ending in a clasp
closed by a screw.

Gold *tahitiya kanthaliya*, necklace
Rajasthan, Bikaner
Nineteenth century

weight: 137 g
length: 30 cm
width, centre pendant: 7 cm
width, side pendant: 4.5 cm

Necklace with three hollow gold pendants. The centre pendant is *dholki*-shaped (a *dholki* is a drum, a musical instrument) and the outer two pendants are *phanki* or fan-shaped. On either side of the central pendant is a *goli* (bead) embellished with a rosette, alternating with gold and blue coloured cotton beads. The long finials, fabricated from gold sheet, depict a rosette, set with blue paste and silver-foiled rock crystal, and an *ara* (bird) with green-foiled rock crystal wings and white coral head. All decorative elements are bordered with tiny pearls.

Further information:
Untracht, *Traditional Jewelry of India*, p.130, illustration 223

Gold *kazhuththu uru,* wedding necklace
South India, Tamil Nadu
Nineteenth century

weight: 155 g
length: 31 cm
length, *thali*: 6.5 cm
length, hand-shaped ornaments: 5.5 cm
length, two round pendants: 5 cm
length, back tassel: 5.5 cm

Traditional gold wedding necklace with a central *thali* or
tirumangalyam strung on a black cord with four hand-shaped
and two round ornaments on either side. These alternate with
fourteen identical cylindrical tubes and four tube-shaped *kolai*,
and a *kunchcham* (back tassel-pendant, tipped with a gold bead)
fixed to the ends of the cords.

The central *thali*, the actual marriage ornament, shows the four-
armed goddess Lakshmi sitting on a lotus-shaped throne with legs
folded. Lakshmi wears a crown and in her two upper hands she
holds a lotus flower, her two lower hands are in a boon-giving
gesture.

*The four hand-shaped ornaments (nalu viralkal) represent the hands of the
couple who are getting married.*

Yellow glass roof finials in the City Palace, Udaipur

Multi-coloured glass *zenana* window in the City Palace, Udaipur

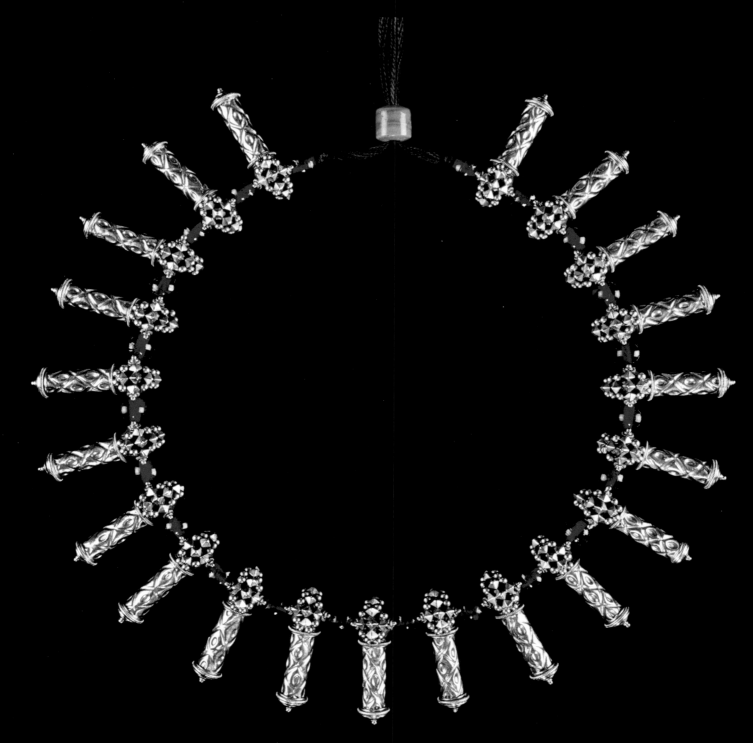

Gold marriage necklace
South India, Kerala
Nineteenth century

total length: 40 cm
length, one gold pod: 4 cm
weight: 200 g

Marriage necklace consisting of twenty-one gold cylindrical pods attached to a black cotton cord, alternated with twenty-two blue spherical glass spacers and one coral bead. The shapes of the gold tubes and the decoration are characteristic of the gold work of southern India. The long tubes are receptacles for charms and mantras.

A noteworthy feature of this necklace is that it combines characteristics of both northern and southern India, a rare phenomenon. An unusual feature of this necklace are the old, blue, glass beads, all of which are in remarkable condition. Old glass, as featured in this necklace, is to be found in great quantities and in all forms in the City Palace of Udaipur, Rajasthan.

After the Sisodia Rajputs had left Chittor, they established themselves and made their capital city in Udaipur. The women's quarters in the palace (the zenana), had walls built with small square open spaces covered with coloured glass. When the women looked out through these small 'windows' the scenery acquired a marvellous technicolour glow. Exquisite coloured glass was also used to decorate the roof finials of the City Palace.

This type of marriage ornament is often worn by the Nambudari, commonly pronounced and written 'Nambari', a Brahman tribe of Malabar, south-west coast of India.

Further information:
Brijbhushan, *Indian Jewellery Ornaments and Decorative Designs*, plate LX

Gold *phanki har,* necklace
Rajasthan, Shekavati area
Nineteenth century

Necklace consisting of four *phanki,* arrowhead or fan-shaped pendants and two tube-shaped finials on either side. In the centre is a triangular *kodagu* pendant. The four pendants are each attached by two loops to a traditional cotton cord, embellished with *kalabattu,* woven cotton balls bedecked with thin gold thread, as spacers. The centre pendant, attached by one loop, depicts the goddess Lakshmi with four arms, sitting on a lotus-shaped throne, wearing short and long necklaces and an impressive crown. The two pendants on either side depict Lord Ganesha with four arms, legs folded, and flanked by two peacocks. The hollow pendants are of a stamped technique.

Fan-shaped pendants are often seen in traditional jewellery from Rajasthan in the Shekawati district.

Gold necklace
Gujarat
Nineteenth century

weight: 157 g
length: 27 cm

The necklace consists of a central container-shaped pendant with an embellishment of an oval and flower theme and seven diamond-shaped finials below. All are set with rubies and diamonds, bordered with tiny seed pearls. On either side of the pendant are twelve gold bird-shaped ornaments, each holding a little ring with gold balls in its beak. The birds are crowned with six tiny gold beads and three circular discs. The bird pendants are soldered to a double diamond-shaped gold unit set with rubies with two loops at the back where two chains pass through. The wax in the bird-shaped pendants and the gold balls is clearly visible on the reverse. Because of the softness of the gold (minimum 23 karat) the wax was required to support the gold.

Pair of gold *gajredar,* bracelets
North-western Rajasthan
Late nineteenth century

Heavy, gold wrist ornaments worn by women. Each bracelet comprises seven half dome-shaped units with a structure formed by innumerable small solid gold balls (*gajre*) held together in their integral loops with gold wire. The bracelets have a threaded-pin opening mechanism.

This traditional work is known as gold ke gajre kam *and is still popular in Rajasthan and Northern India. It is also often seen in silver.*

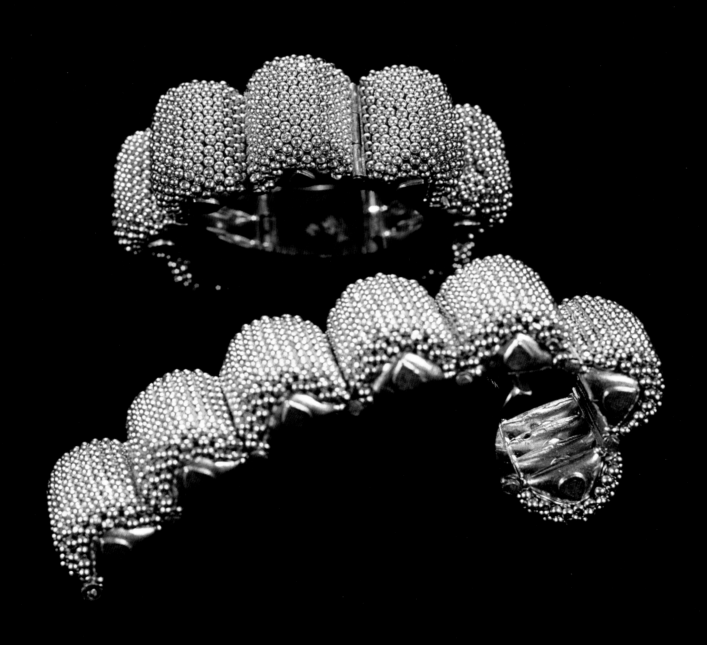

Gold *kattawala gokhru*, earrings
Northern Gujarat, Rajasthan
Twentieth century

The style of earring shown here, which has a loop-type fastening, is seen in Rajasthan (Barmer and Jaisalmer district) and is worn by men of all castes. The design, consisting of spiky hollow balls that are individually soldered to the surface of a hollow gold ball (*babul* technique) is probably inspired by the prickly blossoms of the *babul* flower. The thorny type (*katta* means thorn) *kattawala gokhru* resembles the style of Himachal Pradesh, Shimla district, where they are ordered for marriages and worn by the bride.

The dense babul tree, native to India and Africa, with bright golden-yellow flowers, grows in dry arid areas, and flowers all year round.

Further information:
Ganguly, *Earrings, Ornamental Identity and Beauty in India*, p.116
Barnard, *Indian Jewellery*, p.176

Gold necklace
South India
Late nineteenth/early twentieth century

weight: 82 g
length: 32 cm

Necklace consisting of twenty oblong-shaped gold pendants with a
kirtimukha (face of glory mask) decoration. Half-circular forms are
attached to each pendant, depicting an *apsara* in flight.

*An apsara or apsarasa is a supernatural beautiful and elegant female spirit
in Hindu and Buddhist mythology. As celestial maidens, they inhabit the skies
and are often depicted in flight and appear on temple walls in many different
poses. There are two types of females represented: apsaras and devatas. The
former are always poised ready to dance, the latter standing still and facing
forward in their role as temple guardians. Poets have written about the grace
and loveliness of apsaras, and how they delighted the gods with their dances.
They are described as 'tender maidens with the beauty of the rising moon'.**

The *apsara* below carries a bowl of fruit and holds a large flower
bud in her right hand. She is depicted wearing a *bhor* at her hair
parting, a circular flat ear decoration, and two bangles on each
arm.

* Further information:
Nevile, *Nautch Girls of India*, p.13

Apsara as a wall decoration inside the City Palace, Udaipur.

Gold *mulligai arumbu malai,* necklace
Tamil Nadu
Nineteenth century

Elaborate gold *mulligai arumbu malai,* consisting of forty long,
hollow stylised jasmine buds decorated with the goddess
Lakshmi on the upper part of each unit.

Pair of *khatria*, guard bangles
Rajasthan, Bikaner
Early twentieth century

Flat gold bangles with black dyed ivory bands on the inside and a floral and seed pearl decoration. Thirty-eight units leading to a round gold ball (possibly a flower bud). These bangles are worn on both wrists above and below a series of smaller bangles.

Further information:
Untracht, *Traditional Jewelry of India*, p.180, image 334
Hendley, *Indian Jewellery*, p.15, plate 7, numbers 38, 41

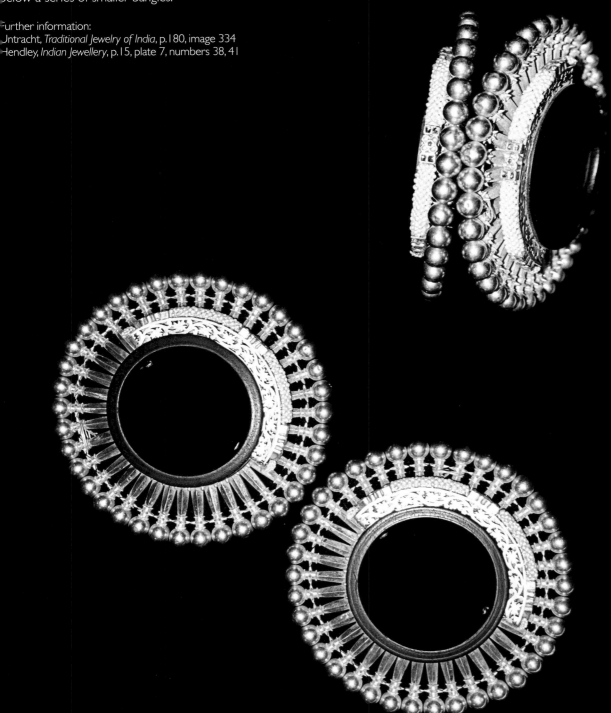

Pair of gold *kara,* bangles
Rajasthan, Ajmer
Nineteenth century

Pair of gold 'knitted' bangles consisting of two parts hinged
together and fabricated solely from a woven loop-in-loop chain. A
slightly curved gold sheet, soldered to the inside of the wire work,
gives support to the hollow tube. Two small bands are attached
to the end of the gold wire to form the screw-post clasp.

Knitted wire work is also seen as anklets, with and without the curved gold
sheet. This type of gold wire work reflects the early Islamic use of knitted tubes.

Further information:
Jenkins and Keene, *Islamic Jewelry in the Metropolitan Museum of Art,*
illustration 23

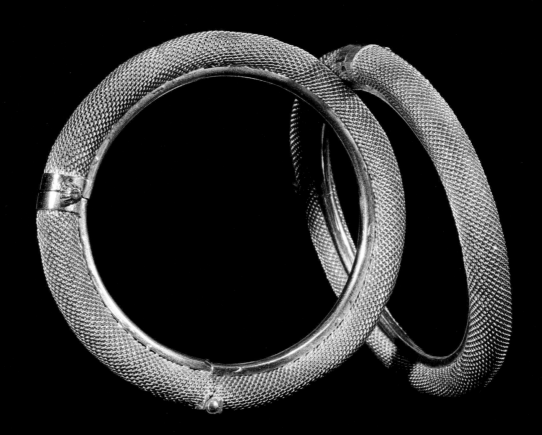

Gold necklace
West Bengal, Calcutta
Early twentieth century

Gold necklace consisting of four lines of floral motif segments, connected through small rings decorated with a tiny floral motif. The four gold chains are attached to three spacers and triangular finials on either side. A pendant with faceted gold studs in a floral pattern is attached to the centre spacer.

Gold bracelet
Tamil Nadu

This bracelet has a double row of stylish mango-shaped links with
gold ball finials. The links are attached to two single loop-in-loop
gold wires at the back.

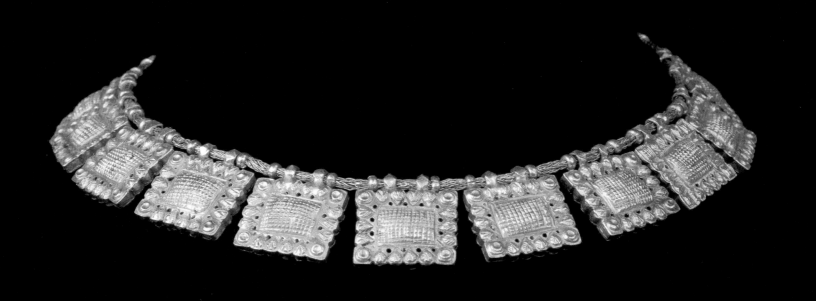

Gold *tabiz*, necklace with square pendants
North India, Rajasthan, Bikaner
Chain, nineteenth century
Tabiz, early twentieth century

High-karat gold, quadruple loop-in-loop chain, with twenty-six gold rings to hold the flexible links together. Thirteen square-shaped *tabiz* (pendants) studded with blue glass paste and *billore* (rock crystal) are attached to the chain. The reverse shows the mirror image of the front in high relief *chitai* work.

Square-shaped short necklaces are often seen on female sculptures as temple architecture.

Gold *phul vedhla,* earrings
Gujarat, Saurashtra and Katchch
Early twentieth century

length: 5.6 cm
weight: 19.8 g

The upper part has a *phul,* a flower design with a rosette in the centre, decorated with granulation work. The lower part of these earrings is related to the *vedhla* worn in the earlobe by the Mer community and is also related to the *loriya* worn in the lobe by married women in the Charan community in western Saurashtra. The *phul vedhla* is worn in the helix by married women of the Rabari, Mer and Dalwara communities, and although it can be worn before marriage, it is usually given to the bride by her in-laws.

Further information:
Weihreter, *Schatze Der Menschen Und Gotter,* p.79, illustration 60

Gold *akota,* ear ornaments
Gujarat, Saurashtra and Kutch
Early twentieth century

Early twentieth-century traditional ear ornaments, primarily worn in the Kutch and Saurasthra regions of Gujarat. The ornaments are decorated from the outside with a fine double row of loop-in-loop wire work, gold discs and single wire. A gold roundel is set in the centre of each, with a gold bead surrounded by six smaller beads decorating the central part of the ornaments. The horizontal band-like decoration at the bottom steadies the weight and prevents sliding.

The earrings are worn in the lobe.

Field information suggests that akota are rare, and where they do occur they are most likely to be formed in silver and worn by the older generation. The gold variety is extremely rare.

Gold *thussi*, necklace
Madhya Pradesh, Indore region
Late nineteenth early twentieth century

Necklace consisting of oblong-shaped loose gold segments, each
set with *pokraj* (white sapphires) foiled rubies and emeralds. The
centre decoration has a crescent and sun motif, set with white
sapphires, rubies and emeralds. Attached to each segment is a
double drop-shaped element, from which a gold wire ring and
small gold beads are suspended. On top of each gold segment is
a double calyx-shaped ornament.

*The calyx-shaped decoration on top would probably have been set
with pearls.*

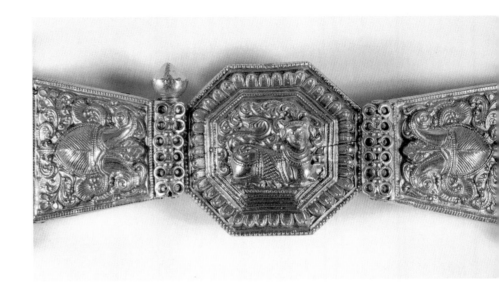

Gold clasp
South India
Late nineteenth century

Gold octagonal centrepiece for a seven-row necklace, depicting a seated Nandi, the bull which serves as the *vahana* (mount) for Lord Shiva. Nandi wears a headdress and several necklaces and is cloaked with a check-design cloth. The centrepiece is flanked on either side by two hinged panels depicting Vaishnavite symbols. The clasp closes with an anti-clockwise screw.

It is believed that Nandi is the bearer of truth and righteousness, he represents faith, constancy in belief and strength and in combination with Lord Shiva is one of the oldest forms in Hindu representation. Nandi sits directly at the entrances to Shiva temples as a guard and protector and unlike other vahanas he is worshipped as a divine figure in his own right. As a separate god, he can be traced back to the Indus Valley civilisation.

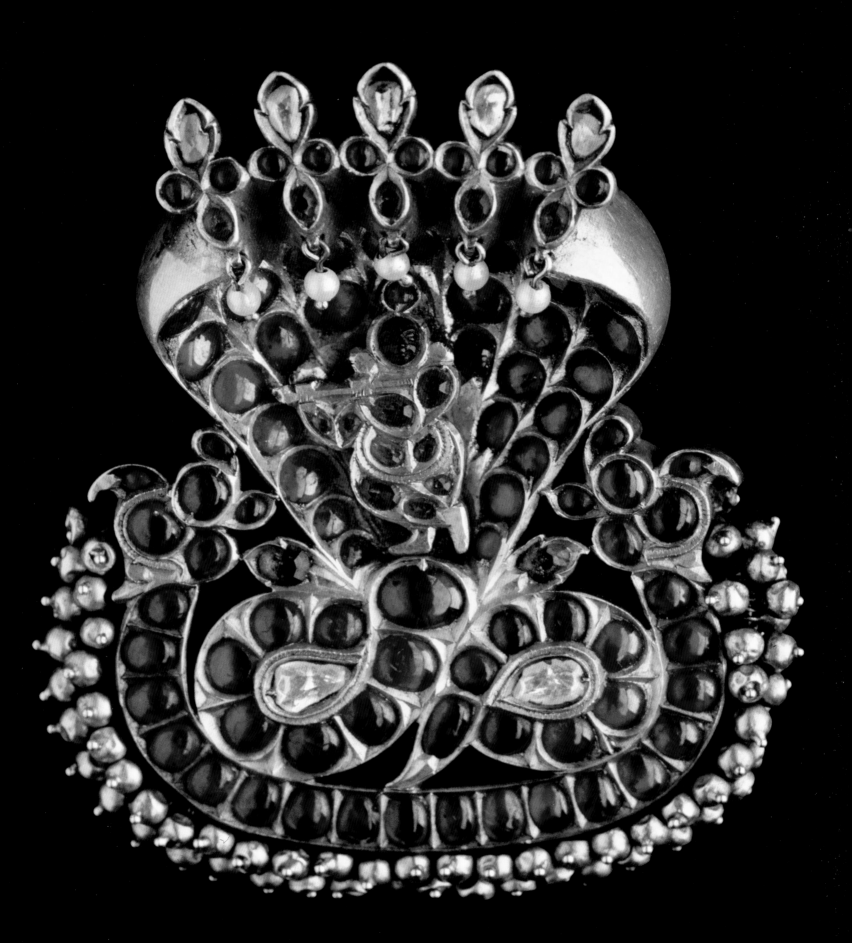

Ruby

Ratna, *Gem of Ravi*

God first created rubies and then created man to posses them

Rubies have been loved for thousands of years in India, and legends circulate that God first created rubies and then created man to possess them. In Hindi, the ruby is referred to as *manak* or *manikya*; the name ruby is derived from the Latin *rubeus* meaning 'red'. In Indian mythology, ruby was given the name *ratna raj*, meaning 'king of jewels' and *Ratnanayaka*, meaning 'Lord of Precious Stones'. *Padmaraga,* or 'red as the lotus', was used to describe the beauty of the stone.

Designated as the king of gemstones because of its symbolic mythological and astrological association with Surya (the sun, the divine light, king of the planets, and centre of our solar system), the ruby is always placed in the centre of the *nava ratna* arrangement. It is believed that the ruby inspires creativity, wisdom and love, and those who donate rubies to honour Krishna are assured of being reborn as an emperor in a future life. In India light-coloured rubies are considered appropriate for women, whereas darker coloured and star rubies are most appropiate for men.

Gold hair ornament
South India, Tamil Nadu
Nineteenth century

Gold upper part of a *jadanaagam* (hair braid ornament), depicting the thousand-headed cobra Shesha (also named Ananta), surmounted by a figure of Krishna dancing on the coiled serpent and holding up his flute to play. Krishna's face is carved from an emerald and his body is set with emeralds; the gold hair ornament, 'crowned' with five diamonds, is set with cabochon-cut Burmese rubies, diamonds and emeralds, and has five pearls suspended at the top.

The depiction of Krishna, the eighth incarnation of Lord Vishnu, is considered to be the most important of the ten incarnations. He represents all aspects of human development from childhood through adolescence to adulthood. Young Krishna is shown standing on one leg with the other crossed in front, while holding his favourite instrument, the flute. The young Krishna depicted in this hair ornament is sheltered by the five-headed serpent King Shesha, who is the king of all nagas (serpent deities). In the Puranas (ancient Hindu text), Shesha is said to hold all the planets of the universe. Sometimes he is also shown as seven-headed, but more commonly as a thousand-headed serpent. His name means 'that which remains', because it is believed that when the world is destroyed at the end of Kalpa, a certain period of time, Shesha will remain as he is.

Ruby is the most valuable red variety in the corundum family, making it, together with sapphire, the second hardest mineral on earth; on the Mohs scale it scores 9 out of 10, just behind diamond. The term corundum is derived from the Sanskrit word *kuruvinda*. Pure corundum (aluminium oxide) is colourless and traces of elements such as aluminium oxide are responsible for the red colour. Only red corundum is entitled to be called ruby, while all other colours are classified as sapphires or 'fancy sapphires'. The most important characteristic of this gem is its amazing (purplish) red colours which varies from transparent pink through rose to deep carmine and its silky and milky inclusions.

Ancient Sanskrit texts name two main sources that would have supplied India with rubies: Burma and Sri Lanka. Somewhat later texts also mention regions in the subcontinent itself: Kalinga (the valleys between the Mahanadi and Godavari rivers in north-east India) and Kalpur (central India), but neither have been important sources of corundum. Rubies found in South India at Kangiyan are of a dull, pale tint and are known as Kangiyan rubies. Rubies have also been mined in former Siam (now Thailand), but they were commonly of a slightly darker colour compared to rubies from the famous Mogok region, Burma. Marco Polo mentioned Sri Lanka in his thirteenth-century travelogue *Il Millione*, as being famous for precious stones in general, and for rubies in particular. He has the following to say about a ruby that once graced the Ruwanwelisaya Dagoba, a stupa at Anuradhapura: 'a flawless ruby, a span long and quite as thick as a man's fist'. Later on he speaks of 'the King of the Coromandel country [eastern coast of Tamil Nadu] wearing golden bracelets set with the richest pearls, necklaces of rubies, emeralds and sapphires, anklets at his feet and gold rings on his toes. He wore a rosary of 104 large rubies and pearls.' Some time later, the Venetian merchant and explorer Nicolo dei Conti (1395–1469) mentioned ruby mining in Burma. From approximately the fifteenth or sixteenth century, ships were laying anchor in ports along the Malabar and Coromandel coasts of South India where Machilipatnam (Masulipatnam) was the centre of the ruby trade from Burma. This activity was dominated mainly by the Chettiar community who traded with the markets and bazaars in South India. The best quality rubies at that time came from the Mogok Valley, located north-east of the city of Mandalay in Upper Burma (now known as Myanmar), and the finest colour is called 'pigeon blood' (*ko-twe* in Burmese), the term being derived from Sanskrit.

Three important factors define the rubies from Upper Burma which are regarded as the finest quality rubies: an intense red colour, strong crimson fluorescence and the presence of tiny rutile fibres, called silk. Particularly large rubies of the most splendid quality are amongst the most valuable minerals known to mankind. In the past, any stones found to be above 5 carats and of good quality were considered the property of the Burmese ruler. The deep crimson-red of a fine Mogok ruby is incomparable. That is how they became the benchmark for top quality rubies today. The rubies were sold by a weight known as the ratti (a bright red and black seed, an old Indian measure used for gems and precious metals because of its uniform weight). One ratti was equivalent to 0.91 carat.

Various travellers and explorers in and around the subcontinent during Mughal times mention other sources of rubies in addition to Burma, as we know from early seventeenth-century documents of the East India Company. Other red gems and semi-precious stones such as red spinel, red garnet, red topaz, rubellite and red tourmaline are similar in colour to the ruby but these stones are all much softer and lighter in weight than rubies. They also lack the ruby's silky and milky inclusions. However, at the time, all the other coloured stones were called rubies and were only differentiated by their colour in the same way as sapphire was called blue ruby, amethyst was then violet ruby, and so on. In Indian culture, ruby was considered to be the king of gemstones for its majesty and colour. Rubies were cherished by royalty and nobility and since the medieval period have been loved by religious leaders. Ideally, rubies are worn on the ring finger. In ancient times Indian society was organised according to a scientific division of human activities and rubies, in the same way as the four *varnas* were divided into categories, on the basis of the professions:

Brahmin, rubies having the colour of pigeon's blood and/or rose petals;
Kshatriya, rubies with the colour of red lotus;
Vaishya, rubies of crimson colour resembling the seeds of pomegranate;
Shudra, rubies having a dirty red colour.

Historians and scholars sometimes identify different categories:

the true oriental ruby, being the Brahmin
the rubicelle, a Kshatriya
the spinel, a Vaishya
the balas-ruby, a Shudra[1]

The seventeenth-century French traveller Jean Baptiste Tavernier (1605–1689) wrote extensively about some of the largest rubies in his book *Travels in India*. However, as every red stone was classified as a ruby at that time it is likely that some of these stones were spinel (balas ruby).

Peace Ruby

The Reverend Father Sangermano (1758–1819), who lived for 23 years as a missionary in Ava, the capital of Burma (today Inwa, Myanmar), noted in his book *The Burmese Empire a Hundred Years Ago*, that: 'it is the Rubies of the Burmese Empire which are its greatest boast, as both in brilliance and clearness they are the best in the world.' J. F. Halford-Watkins mentioned that the famous Peace Ruby (rough stone, 42 carats), discovered on 30 June 1919 in the mines of the Mogok Valley, was a magnificent stone and at that time the finest ruby the world had ever seen. After cutting and polishing in Bombay the Peace Ruby had a weight of 25 carats. Unfortunately the present location of the Peace Ruby is unknown.

The Chhatrapati Manik Ruby

A magnificent oval cabochon-cut ruby of a deep red colour. The source of the stone is questionable, as is its exact size—estimated to have been over 20 carats. Throughout history, scholars have suggested different places as its origin: is it possible that the Chhatrapati Manik originated from India itself, or is its source Burma or Sri Lanka?

Its history dates back almost 2,000 years to the rule of the powerful emperor of northern India, King Chandragupta II, also known as Vikramaditya of Ujjain. He proclaimed himself as Chhatrapati, Supreme King. Upon advice from his astrologers, he had the stone placed in the centre of his crown. Over generations, the ruby passed through various hands into the treasury of Mughal emperor Aurengzeb (ca. 1687) who was so impressed by its beauty that he ordered his name to be engraved on it. Later, he presented the stone to a very loyal and renowned family of bankers who lived in Murshidabad in Bengal. A merchant from Lucknow named Lala Kalkadas purchased the Chhatrapati Manik from the banker's family and decided to remove the seal of Aurengzeb from the stone, not realising its historical significance. His son Lala Budreedas inherited the historic ruby and had it remounted as a centrepiece in a new tiara. The Chhatrapati Manik reappeared in London in 1934 as the centrepiece of an aigrette on a diamond tiara, but since then its whereabouts are unknown.

Star Ruby

Traditionally, star rubies were worn by knights in the battlefield to protect themselves from the enemy. The power of a star ruby is said to be at its highest during a full moon. Local tales in Karnataka say that if a ruby is worn as a visible pendant or as headgear, then anyone who faces you as an enemy will lose half his valour. Star rubies are precious rarities and should always display sharp rays of reflected light which are fully formed all the way to the imaginary horizontal line that runs through the middle of the stone, and the star itself should be situated right in the centre. Star rubies usually have a six-pointed three-ray star, but it may have four to twelve rays depending on the crystal system of the gem, and should be silvery or milky white. Generally the best star effect (asterism) is found only in corundum from Burma and Sri Lanka which contains sufficient amounts of aligned rutile needles in the corundum. To display the star effect in the best way, the ruby is cut as a cabochon with a round- or oval-shaped dome. In general, a star ruby is more pinkish than deep red.

Famous Star Rubies

One of the world's largest and finest star rubies (138.7 carat) is the Rosser Reeves Ruby, which was donated by Mr Reeves to the Smithsonian Institute in Washington, DC in 1965. This magnificent stone, found at a Sri Lankan mine, is almost translucent and displays a six-rayed star.

The DeLong star ruby (100.32 carat), a deep purplish red oval cabochon-cut six-rayed star ruby, found in Burma was donated by Mrs Edith Haggin de Long to the American Museum of Natural History in New York in 1937.

The prosperity and wealth of south India have helped it to maintain the rich heritage of its jewellery tradition. In the south of India, the use of rubies in traditional jewellery was and still is exuberant, due to the flourishing trade undertaken by the Chettiar community. Although all kinds of precious stones are available, it is mainly ruby set in gold that prevails, sometimes combined with diamonds, emeralds or pearls. The rubies used in southern Indian style jewellery are small, because most rubies are on average less than a quarter of a carat. They are tumbled to create their round form; sometimes they are rectangular in shape and usually flat on one side. Because of their natural quality and beauty they did not need any other shaping; polishing on the surface was sufficient. In Tamil Nadu (South India), the rubies used in jewellery are cabochon rubies, also known as *kuruvindam*, from which the English word 'corundum' is derived. Style-wise, jewellery design and shape tended not to be influenced by fashion. Centuries-old traditions are followed and more often than in any other part of the country, pieces of jewellery were handed down from great-grandmother to grandmother to mother to daughter. This explains why jewels from the south tend to be more traditional.

Another specific feature in South India was the use of a red stone called kemp or *kempukal*. Kemp is a mineral that is found along the riverbeds of the Manjra river in Bidar district in Karnataka. The red stone is often found set in temple jewellery that has been donated to a temple to adorn the idol of a god or goddess, but these images are also seen adorned with beautiful gold jewellery and studded with real rubies. One of the oldest dance forms in India is Bharata Natyam, and in it the dancers, male and female, wear a unique type of temple jewellery which is often set with kempukal stones.

1. Kunz, *The Curious Lore of Precious Stones*, p.102.

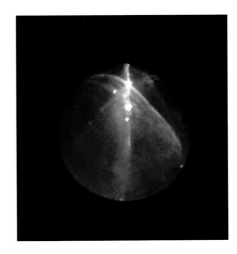

The Rosser Reeves Ruby
© 2017 National Museum of Natural History, National Gem Collection, Smithsonian

Gold necklace with pendants set with rubies, white sapphires and emeralds
Tamil Nadu, probably Chennai
Nineteenth century

Necklace consisting of gold, stylised, mango-shaped ornaments, with nine different shaped gold pendants on either side (each with a different Vaishnavite symbolic meaning), and one crescent-shaped central pendant, all set with cabochon-cut rubies, emeralds and white sapphires. From the half-moon shaped central pendant hangs a circular pendant depicting a *hamsa* (mythical swan or goose). The nine pendants represent symbols of Lord Vishnu; the *hamsa* in the central pendant represents the mythical swan or goose, the mount of Lord Brahma.

Gold toe rings
Andhra Pradesh
Nineteenth century

Two pairs of gold toe rings (*bicchwa* or *nakhlia*) *kundan*-set with rubies and one diamond in the centre. A small anti-clockwise screw makes it possible to open the rings.

Usually, toe rings are worn in pairs on the second toe of both feet, but some bicchwa sets have pairs for all toes. It is preferable that each toe ring has a different myriad decoration. They can also be attached to the payal (foot ornament) that might cover the entire foot from ankle to toes. Traditionally in some parts of India a bicchwa was worn on the big toe of the left foot to indicate a married status.

Hindus consider gold to be the metal of the gods, and because of its respected status it may not be worn below the waist; the exception is royalty, who are permitted to wear gold foot decorations. The Ramayana recounts that Sita, when abducted by Ravana, threw her toe ring away, so that Lord Rama could find her.

Pair of gold fish-shaped ornaments
North India
Nineteenth century

Flexible gold fish-shaped ornaments *kundan*-set with cabochon
rubies, *polki* diamonds and a cabochon emerald.

Gold flexible bracelet
Rajasthan and Gujarat
Nineteenth century

Flexible tube-style knitted gold wire bracelet, *bala*, composed
of many small links closely united together. The large gold clasp
supports the two parts of the bracelet and opens by turning the
screw in an anti-clockwise direction. The whole is set with flat-cut
diamonds, cabochon rubies and emeralds.

Further information:
Untracht, *Traditional Jewelry of India*, p.252, illustration 570

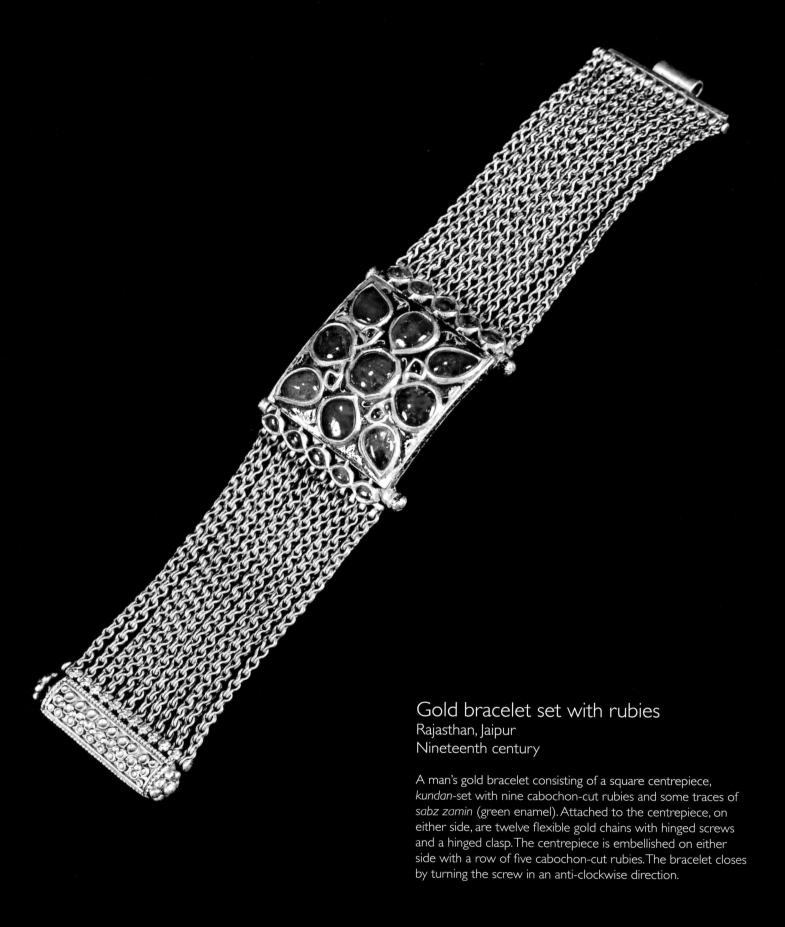

Gold bracelet set with rubies
Rajasthan, Jaipur
Nineteenth century

A man's gold bracelet consisting of a square centrepiece,
kundan-set with nine cabochon-cut rubies and some traces of
sabz zamin (green enamel). Attached to the centrepiece, on
either side, are twelve flexible gold chains with hinged screws
and a hinged clasp. The centrepiece is embellished on either
side with a row of five cabochon-cut rubies. The bracelet closes
by turning the screw in an anti-clockwise direction.

The reverse of the bracelet shows an exquisite enam[el]
in a red and green floral design on a white enamel
background. In the centre there is a red cartouche
bordered with dark blue enamel and traces of white
and gold dots. A white-enamelled dancing pigeon wi[th]
spread tail on a red-enamelled background decorate[s the]
cartouche. Four red-enamelled birds are elegantly pla[ced]
above and below the cartouche. The edges show tra[ces]
of green enamel, the hinges on either side show trac[es]
of blue enamel. The opaque white enamelling, (safed
chalwan) is on a gold surface in the champlevé techn[ique].

The design of the five-petalled flowers with the folia[ge]
and a bird in the centre in combination with the colo[ur]
blue makes it typical Bikaneri School.

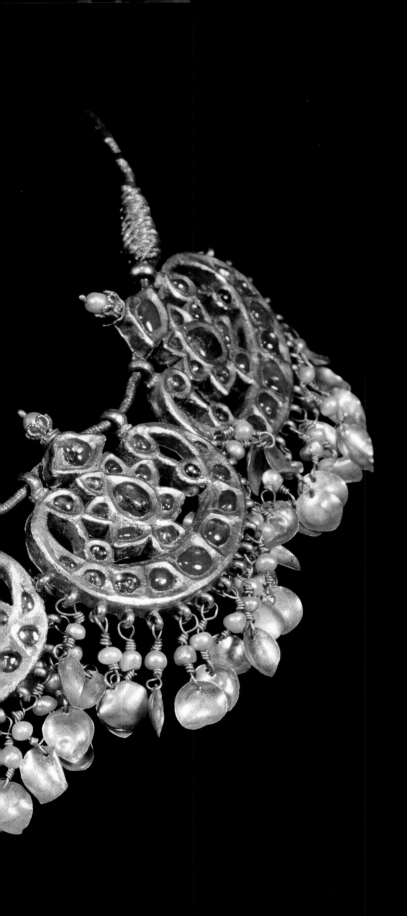

Necklace
Punjab
Nineteenth century

weight: 132 g
width of pendant: 4 cm

Six gold pendants strung on a cord form the necklace. Each
pendant has a pearl on top and is set with cabochon rubies and a
cabochon emerald in the centre, and also shows a stylish crescent
with scrolled terminals and a sun symbol. Suspended from each
pendant is a loop holding a pearl and a *pipal patti* (leaf form).

Pipal patti are the leaves of the Ficus religiosa, *also known in India and
Nepal as the peepal tree or ashwattha tree. This tree is considered sacred
by the followers of Hinduism, Jainism and Buddhism where it is called the
Boddhi tree.*

Gold *rakodi*, head ornament
South India, Tamil Nadu
Nineteenth century

An elaborate circular gold *rakodi* (head ornament) placed on the back of the top of the head. The *rakodi*, with a *hamsa* (swan) in the centre, is *kundan*-set (similar to the *kundan* technique in northern India) with cabochon rubies (also known as *kuruvincam* stones), diamonds and emeralds. The *rakodi* is embellished with a gold decoration of birds and flowers and a fringe of *gajre* (small balls) below.

In Hinduism, hamsa *(or swan) is often associated with wisdom, creativity, beauty and grace and it represents the presence of divine inspiration in our world. In Indian mythology the* hamsa *is the vehicle of Brahma, god of creation.*

Gold *tikka*
South India
Nineteenth century

Gold *tikka*, forehead ornament in a crescent
and floral design, set with cabochon rubies,
emeralds and a diamond in the centre.

Pair of gold flexible bracelets
Gujarat, Baroda
Nineteenth century

Pair of gold flexible bracelets, *kundan*-set with
cabochon rubies and bordered with seed pearls.

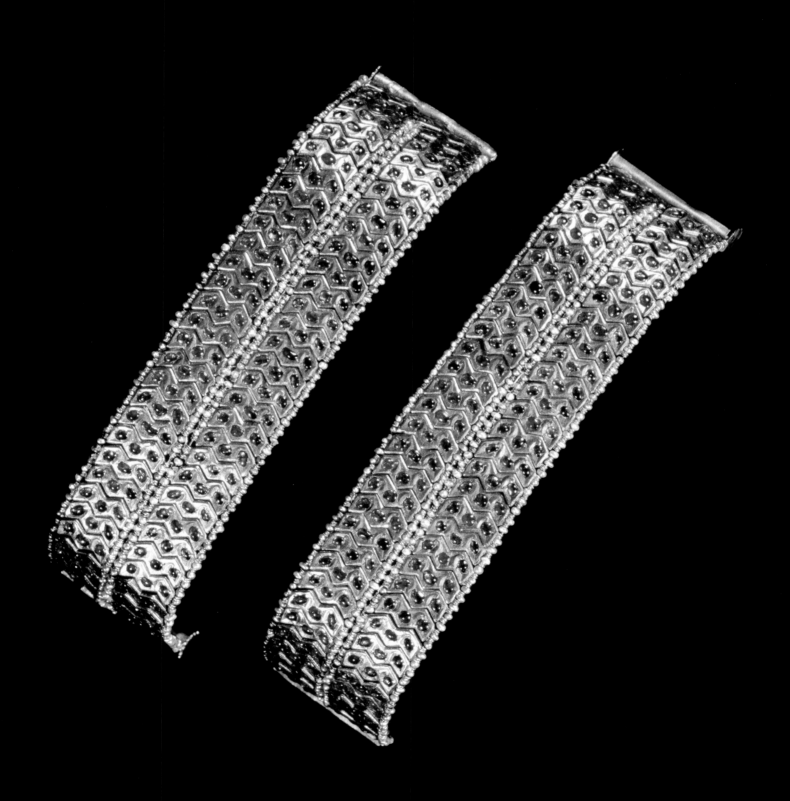

Rakodi, head ornament
Tamil Nadu
Early nineteenth century

An openworked gilded silver crescent-shaped head ornament,
kundan-set with cabochon rubies, emeralds and flat-cut diamonds.
Attached on top are three pearls and a semicircular decoration
of gold beads around the edge.

*The gilded silver is worked in a method known in South India as izhuppuvelai,
where the metal is etched and the stones are set in the base. This jewel
symbolises the moon. It is worn by women at the back of the head as part of
a talaisaman of three head ornaments.*

Further information:
Bala Krishnan and Kumar, *Dance of the Peacock*, p.180, illustration 282,
image on the right-hand side
Van Gelder, *The Origin of Quality*, p.37

Nath, nose ring
Old Punjab, Lahore, Amritsar
Nineteenth century

Gold nose ring in the form of an elegantly curved fish carrying a bird (peacock), *kundan*-set with cabochon rubies, turquoises, and multicoloured moonstones with white and turquoise glass beads suspended below. The upper part on either side has a stylised bird design set with turquoises, cabochon rubies and pearls. The small pendant flower in the centre is set with turquoises and moonstones on different coloured foils.

This specific design 'fish carrying a peacock' is worn by women of the Sikh community in the Punjab. Designs with different birds are worn by women in the Muslim community in Uttar Pradesh. The chain that supported the weight is missing.

Gold *gajra*, bracelet
Rajasthan, Ajmer
Nineteenth century

Seven gold rigid parts, ornamented with gold balls (*gajre*), linked
together to form a bracelet with a two-part hinged clasp stylised in
the form of two parrots set with rubies, emeralds, dark-blue glass
paste and heart-shaped *billore* (rock crystal on foil). Turning the
gold screw anti-clockwise opens the bracelet.

Gold *manga malai*, necklace
South India, Tamil Nadu
Nineteenth century

length: 23 cm
mango-shaped pendant: 2.2 x 1.5 cm

Elaborate gold necklace consisting of thirty-six mango-shaped
segments each set with a central table-cut diamond, encircled
by eight cabochon-cut rubies and topped with a square gold
ruby-set segment. The mango-shaped units are strung on a heavy
gold herring-bone chain alternated with a single flower set in the
centre with a flat-cut diamond and surrounded by five cabochon-
cut rubies. All diamonds and rubies are set in the *kundan*
technique The delicate screw fastening consists of a floral design
set with rubies and diamonds.

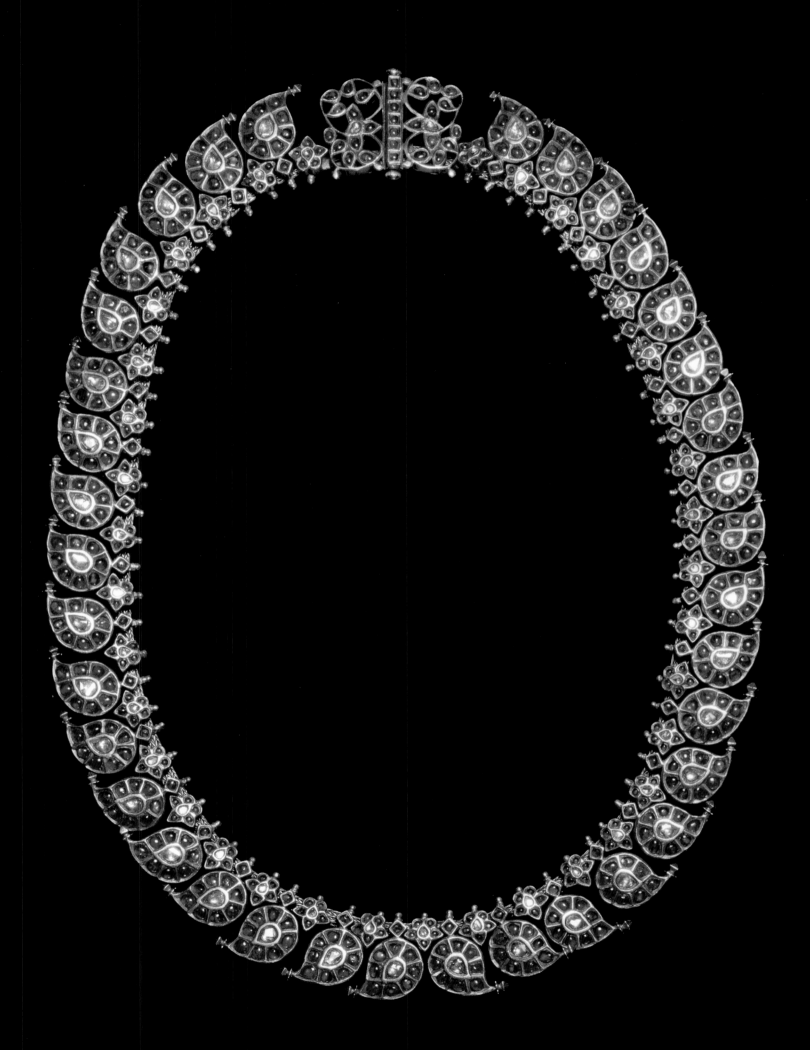

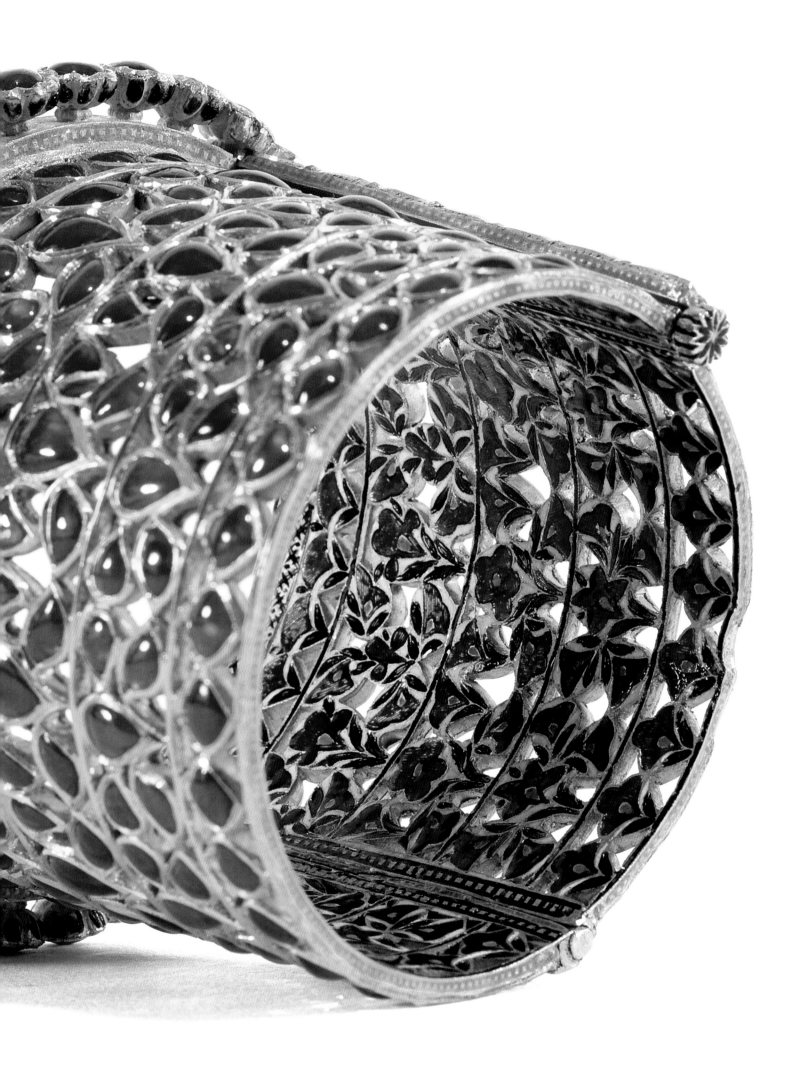

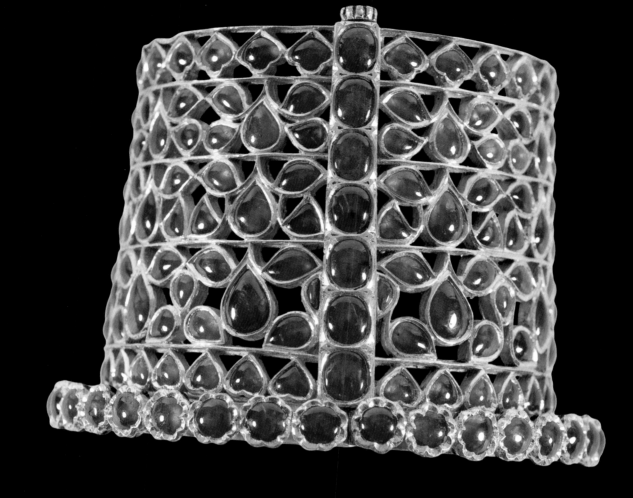

Gold *kada*, cuff
Rajasthan, Bikaner

weight: 276 g
height: 8 cm

Elaborate two-part, hinged gold *kada* (cuff) set with
cabochon rubies and exquisite enamel work on the
inside. The cuff opens by means of a removable pin.

Pair of *zhangfei,* ear ornaments
Upper Assam
Nineteenth century

This impressive pair of ear cylinders or *nadaung* called *zhangfei* originated from the early ear cylinders of Burma. They are made of burmite, also called Burmese amber. The burmite is decorated in gold with *kundan*-set cabochon rubies. The green-enamelled 'star' alternated with the cabochon rubies is seen from the back of the ear lobe.

Further information: Waltraud Ganguly, *Earring: Ornamental Identity and Beauty in India.* p.61; Hendley, *The Rulers of India and Chiefs of Rajputana,* p.143 and plate 136, illustrations 977, 978; plate 137, illustration 981.

Burmite, or Burmese amber, from the Hukawng Valley in the northern state of Kachin in Burma, is the fossilised sap or resin of extinct trees that were growing in the temperate and subtropical forests some sixty million years ago. It is considered to be one of the oldest and hardest fossiliferous ambers known and is found all over the world. It is also one of the most beautiful of all gem-grade ambers. Amber is generally translucent pale yellow, to orange, reddish and dark brown in colour; Burmese amber with its deep red colour and high fluorescent quality is the rarest and most valuable.

Further information:
Grimaldi, *Amber,* p.194

One of the great events in a girl's life is the ceremony of ear-boring, nadwin mingala. Sometimes taking place as early as six or seven years old, but more commonly when she reaches puberty, at the age of twelve or thirteen. Before this ceremony takes place, girls are prohibited from wearing any important gold jewellery or ornaments. A reference to the girl's horoscope shall point out the auspicious day and the propitious moment to puncture the ear lobes. This is performed by a professional ear-borer using large sharp-pointed silver nails; silver is used even in the poorest communities. For the more privileged girls the needles are gold and often adorned with jewels. The needles remain in the ear lobes and are moved several times a day until the little wounds are sufficiently healed, at which point the needles can be withdrawn. The holes are filled with smooth thin stalks of grass and the slow process of enlargement can begin by adding one stalk every day until the opening in the lobe is large enough to accommodate the full-sized ear-cylinder. This takes time because the ordinary ear-cylinder (nadaung) is about 2.5 to 3 cm long and has an average diameter of approximately 1.5 cm, but can be a little thinner in the middle. Ear-cylinders come in different sizes.

Further information:
Dautremer, *Burma under British Rule—and Before*, pp.201, 202

Pair of gold flexible bracelets
Rajasthan, Bikaner
Nineteenth century

This exquisite pair of flexible bracelets consists of a series of interlocking gold links set with three rows of cabochon rubies attached to a rigid upper part in the form of two *makara*-head terminals. The heads are also *kundan*-set with cabochon rubies. Between them they hold in their mouths a magical circular bead-form jewel, which is covered with red and gold enamel. The bracelet fastening is an anti-clockwise screw on top of the magical bead, set with a cabochon ruby. The long and upturned snouts show pink enamel and large white-enamelled teeth. Both heads are *sabz zamin* (green-enamelled) on top with opaque white dots and powder-blue (*ab-e-lehr*, representing waves—the *makara* is a mythical sea creature) enamel on the lower part with a *lal zamin* (red-enamelled) tear-shaped decoration.

We come across the mythical sea creature makara *in various cultures, particularly in early China. The dragon is said to be the emblem of vigilance, the safeguard and guardian of treasures. The appurtenance of the* makara *is variously described as the sun, the moon, the symbol of rolling thunder, and a shining pearl. The Chinese imperial coat of arms from the Han to the Ching dynasty consisted of a pair of dragons holding a pearl. The* makara *has featured on the ceremonial flags of the peoples of the* karava *caste in Sri Lanka since the fourteenth century. In Hindu mythology this sea creature is generally depicted as (front) part terrestrial animal such as crocodile, elephant or deer, and (hind) part aquatic animal. Lord Vishnu is sometimes shown wearing* makarakundalas *(makara-shaped earrings). Makara sculptures are also found as protectors above portals to temples.*

Further information:
India: jewels that enchanted the world, p.221, image 124

Gold ornaments
North India

A pair of gold ornaments representing birds, set with
ten different weight cabochon-cut foiled rubies and
nine table-cut and foiled diamonds.

Head ornament
West Bengal, Kolkata, ca. 1900

A transparant pink and light-blue enamelled gold and silver head decoration in the form of three snakes, set with diamonds and rubies.

In Hindu mythology, three coilled snakes symbolise the past, present and future. Lord Shiva is depicted in many images wearing a garland of snakes (cobras) prominently around his neck, signifying that he is the master of time and energy.

It is said that when snakes are depicted wearing rubies and diamonds on their head, that those precious gems serve as lampes for Lord Shiva and his consort Paravati.

This ornament could have embellished a Shiva statue.

Pearl
Mukta, *Gem of Chandra*

Pearls alone are to be found within living organisms,
owing nothing to man—they are a gift from nature

Pearls have featured prominently throughout the history of traditional Indian jewellery, and no gem has been more prolifically used than the pearl (*moti* or *mukta*). In *nava ratna* philosophy, the pearl is associated with the moon, personified as the deity Chandra, and is one of the five great gems, the *maharatnani* (diamond, emerald, ruby, sapphire and pearl).

It is believed that the pearl was the first gem to be discovered by man and it is mentioned in many ancient texts as being the oldest of the Vedas, the *Rig-Veda*. In the Mahabharata and Ramayana, a pearl is a gift from the sea to the gods. Legends and stories about pearls being prized above all other gems are many, and of the nine important (*nava ratna*) gems, pearls alone are to be found within living organisms, owing nothing to man—they are a gift from nature.

Pearls are produced by different species of salt and freshwater molluscs (soft-bodied animals protected by a hard exterior shell). The best-known pearl-producing molluscs are the so-called 'pearl-oysters', belonging to a group of molluscs known as bivalves and the *Pinctada* genus. For natural pearls to develop, a tiny foreign body must find its way inside a shell and lodge there. If the mollusc is unable to get rid of this impurity then it begins to secrete a substance called conchiolin, to soothe the irritation and protect itself. A whitish substance called nacre is secreted over the conchiolin. Nacre is the same iridescent substance found lining the insides of shells and is composed of calcium carbonate crystals. When sufficient layers have formed, and when the crystals are properly aligned, an iridescent effect is created as light travels through

Gold *chuda*, bangle
Rajasthan, Bikaner and Shekawati area
Nineteenth century

Gold *chuda* (bangle), *kundan*-set with diamonds, rubies and emeralds, and decorated with pearls.

Traditionally women in Rajasthan wear sets of eight bangles of different sizes called *chuda*. The smallest bangles are called *chudii*, the slightly bigger bangles are called *chhand*, and the biggest are called *pachelli*. This bangle is a rare example of a series of joined bangles.

Emperor Akbar's Baroque Pearl
Drop Pendant
Sixteenth century
© The Museum of Islamic Art, Doha, Qatar

each layer. This is referred to as the pearl's lustre. The thicker the nacre and more perfectly aligned each crystal layer, the more beautiful, rare and valuable the pearl. It may take ten years or more to grow a pearl six millimetres in diameter. The result also depends on the genus of the oyster and its environment. The shape of the pearl is determined by the shape of the foreign body, its position within the shell and the build-up of the layers of nacre enveloping the foreign body.

Pearls are composed of an organic substance, it is therefore impossible to predict a precise lifespan. Some estimates suggest an average of 110–250 years. However, there are pearls that are several hundred years old and still look glorious, and careful maintenance can most certainly help maintain a pearl's quality. A good example of a pearl with a known lifespan is the baroque pearl known as Emperor Akbar's Baroque Pearl Drop Pendant, which dates from the late sixteenth century. It is a large, oval-shaped, slightly baroque pearl, approximately four centimetres in diameter, with an enamelled gold cap featuring a leaf motif engraved on top; on one of the leaves appear the numerals 982, in Arabic, indicating the date in the Islamic calendar (AD 1574, Gregorian calendar). The date on the gold cap encompasses the period of the third great Mughal emperor, Jalaluddin Muhammad Akbar, whose reign extended from 1556 to 1605. This pearl pendant is the earliest known example of a dated piece of Mughal jewellery. During an auction held in London in 1999, the baroque pearl was on view but the owner of the pearl pendant was not identified, nor was the identity of the purchaser revealed.

Another extravagant use of pearls can be seen in the 173 × 264-centimetre Pearl Carpet of Baroda, part of a set originally comprising four rectangular carpets and a circular canopy, commissioned in 1860 by the Maharaja Khanderao Gaekwad of Baroda (1856–1870). The carpet got its name from the Maratha Princely State of Baroda (today Vadodara, Gujarat) and was referred to as a pearl carpet because of the abundance of more than a million natural *khakh* or *buka* seed pearls, and various precious gems such as diamonds, emeralds and rubies. The carpet was completed in 1865, and was intended as a cover for the tomb of the Holy Prophet of Islam, Prophet Muhammad, in Medina. Gaekwad Khanderao was a Hindu ruler, but was fascinated by Islam and ordered the carpet in order to fulfil a vow, and as a mark of his respect for Islam. Unfortunately he passed away before he could deliver the carpet, which then remained as a state treasure. The splendid carpet was displayed at the Delhi Exhibition in 1902 and at the Metropolitan Museum of Art, New York, in 1985. In 2009 the carpet was auctioned and sold to an anonymous telephone buyer. Currently the amazing carpet and Emperor Akbar's baroque pearl are displayed in the Museum of Islamic Art at Doha, Qatar.

Italian fountains outside the Durbar Hall of Lakshmi Vilas, the royal residence of the Maharaja Sayajirao Gaekwad III

Also from the Royal Treasury of the Maharaja of Baroda came the legendary necklace, composed of seven strands of perfectly matched natural pearls, graduated according to size, shape, colour, lustre and surface quality, which came to be known as the Seven-Strand Baroda Pearl Necklace. After Indian Independence in 1947, the government issued an ultimatum to the Maharaja to return the Crown Jewels to the Baroda Treasury. At that time the necklace was reduced to five strands from its original seven and it was stipulated that the pearl necklace be kept in Lakshmi Vilas Palace in Vadodara (early Baroda), the official residence of the Royal Family of Baroda.

The roundness of a pearl is important, as is the fact that a pearl is free from irregularities and blemishes; all these qualities influence its value. Pearls with an irregular shape (that is, not perfectly round) are called baroque pearls and the most sought after are the pear-shaped ones. Pearls are the only gem that do not require any finishing process to bring out their natural beauty, they only need to be drilled to be used as a jewel. The drilling, done by hand, according to a three-thousand-year-old method that requires great skill and delicacy, was and still is, a hereditary occupation, and the best borers, still found in Mumbai, have the ability to drill the very smallest of seed pearls. Compared with other gems, pearls are not very hard, they typically read 2.5–3.5 on the Mohs scale, but their compact nature makes them resistant and durable.

As with precious gems, Hindu culture groups pearls according to the four established *varnas*. The Brahmins, or the learned ones, are an intellectual class that advise on religious, spiritual and political matters; their colour is white. The warrior class, the Kshatriya, guard the social structure against outside aggression; their colour is pink. The trader class, the Vaishya, carry out various occupations in the field of exchange of commodities; their colour is yellow. The service class, the Shudra, perform small services; their colour is black. [1]

In India, for many centuries, the most important sources of natural pearls were the sandbanks off the island of Bahrain in the Persian Gulf and the waters of the Gulf of Mannar, between the north-west coast of Sri Lanka and the south-east coast of India. The Red Sea and the Indian Ocean also supported enormous oyster banks. Natural pearls that came from the Far East were termed oriental pearls. From the waters of the Persian Gulf, where the oldest and most prolific pearl banks in the world were located, pearls came to shore at the harbour city Basra, hence the name 'Basra pearls'. The fisheries of the Bay of Bengal yielded a more rose-coloured pearl which was more globular and softer than the Basra pearl. Natural pearls, found in wild oysters, came from all these areas. After harvesting, the pearls were washed, cleaned and selected according to size by passing them through a series of brass sieves and graded by shape, colour and lustre, and finally valued. The weight of pearls was given in 'grain' (0.05 grain = 0.25 carat).

Until the fifteenth century the pearl trade was dominated mainly by Arabs and Persians, who shipped the pearls to India. That changed after the Portuguese fleet under the command of Vasco da Gama (1460–1524) arrived in 1498 in Kappadu (Kerala) near Calicut (present-day Kozhikode) on the west coast of India. After a short time the Portuguese also colonised Goa and Bon Bahia (present day Mumbai), knowing that the land would supply all manner of gems, exotic products, spices and fabrics. From the sixteenth century, the largest trade in pearls and gemstones in Asia operated from Goa and later also from Mumbai. The Portuguese controlled the great pearl fisheries and trade for nearly a century.

Important pearls were always a major trading commodity and helped to finance the acquisition of all kinds of luxury goods, such as gold, silk, precious stones, coral and ivory. Sometimes tributes and ransoms were paid with pearls and precious stones. After about a century, the Persians expelled the Portuguese and made the Gulf area the world's leading pearl producer during the eighteenth century.

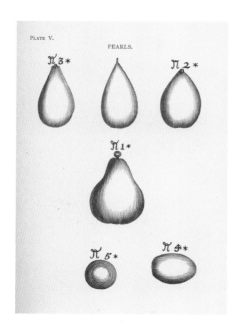

Excerpts from Tavernier, *Travels in India*

Niccolao Manucci (1639–1717) describes in his '*Storia Do Mogor* or Mogul India', written between 1653 and 1708, the seed-pearl fisheries of Tuticorin (Storia I, 59): The Dutch controlled the pearl fishing in the waters between Ceylon and the coast of Tutochorim (present day Tuticorin Tamil Nadu). They issued licences to fish for twenty-one days, starting at the end of March and ending at the end of May. Six hundred *toni* vessels participated, each with a crew of thirty men who paid the Dutch six *patacas* (12 rupees) a head if they were Christian, nine if they were Hindu and twelve if they were Muslim. The Christian boats held three hundred men, those of the Hindus one hundred and the Mohammedans' two hundred; eighteen thousand men in total, all of whom were divers. Many more people were involved as traders and carriers, including women and children, bringing a total of some forty thousand people into the fishery during the season. The naked divers with their bodies oiled, ears stuffed with cotton and nostrils compressed by an instrument made of animal horn, immersed themselves in the water. A few divers used breathing tubes to lengthen their dives. (Leonardo da Vinci illustrated the use of breathing tubes by Indian pearl divers in his *Codice Atlantico*.) With a rope tight around the waist and another rope with a heavy stone attached to his ankle or toe, to hasten his descent, he would have a basket or net hung across his shoulder and hold a *coita* hook in his hand, which he used to detach any shells that may have been stuck to stones. The diver continued to put oysters in the net for as long as he was able to hold his breath; when this was done, he tugged the rope around his waist as a sign to his companions in the vessel to haul him up as fast as possible. This continued every day from sunrise until midday, diver after diver.

Early travellers such as Niccolao Manucci, François Bernier, Jean-Baptiste Tavernier and William Hawkins have given us precious information about customs in India, daily life and wealth at the royal courts. They all wrote about lavish presents, the precious gems and pearls that entered the Mughal treasury. It was Sir Thomas Roe (1615–1619), ambassador of King James to the court of Emperor Jehangir, who complained in his writings to the East India Company, that the king would not receive him without first having received generous presents of pearls and precious stones.[2] We read in *The Shah Jahan Nama*, the written history of Shah Jahan, that a feast was held on the occasion of Jahanara's recovery from a long illness lasting eight months and eight days. On the opening day of the feast the Emperor (her father) bestowed on her 130 unbored pearls for a dast band (bracelet). Jean-Baptiste Tavernier refers to the famous Peacock Throne of which, in his opinion, the most costly part was the twelve columns supporting the canopy, surrounded by rows of beautiful pearls. In his *Travels in India*, Volume I, p.137, he mentions 'a grand bouquet of nine large pear-shaped pearls, of which the largest was thirty carats and the least sixteen, with another single pear-shaped pearl of fifty-five carats.' Can this pearl be the one that Tavernier sold on his final journey to Sháistá Khán, uncle of the great Moghul Aurengzeb and Governor of Bengal? In Volume II, Tavernier describes five more pearls, 'among them the largest and most perfect ever discovered.' Volume II contains a drawing of five amazing pearls, among them (in drawing No.3) a 55-carat pearl. The pearl (drawing No.5) is described as 'a round pearl of perfect forms, this is the largest I know, and it belongs to the Great Moghul.'

Statues of Hindu deities were often adorned with dazzling pearl jewellery such as earrings, bracelets and anklets, and many exquisite miniatures depict emperors, other royals and noblemen wearing important pearl headdresses, turban pearl ornaments, large pearl earrings, pearl bracelets and *bazubands*, and multiple rows of long necklaces of extraordinary lengths bearing pearls of amazing sizes.

Another important reference to pearls and their beauty and lustre is the Moti Masjid, located in Lal Quila, Red Fort in Delhi, built by Emperor Aurengzeb (1659–1660). *Moti* is the Urdu name for 'pearl' and *masjid* is the Urdu name for 'mosque'. As the dome of the mosque was covered in pure white marble, resembling the white lustre of a large pearl, it was called Moti Masjid. It was an established practice to name important mosques after gemstones: Mina Masjid (Gem Mosque) and Nagina Masjid (Jewel Mosque) are both located in Agra Fort in Agra and were completed in 1637 during Emperor Shah Jahan's reign. He also built a Moti Masjid inside Lahore Fort in Lahore Pakistan. In Delhi, near Ajmeri Gate, there is another Moti Masjid, built by the last Mughal emperor, Bahadur Shah II (1837–1857).

Little remains of the once great pearl-fishing industry, as extensive fishing, pollution and oil drilling weakened even the most remote pearl banks. This eventually caused the unfortunate diminishing of this ancient culture. It wiped out the great pearl fisheries and their demise marked the advent of Mikimoto's cultured pearls in the international market.

However, the demand for pearls as jewellery remained and traders from India, where the harvesting of natural pearls since ca. 1900 had almost died out, were soon convinced that they needed to start purchasing *keshi* pearls from Japan. Because they had access to their own Indian labour who had been sorting, drilling and stringing tiny pearls for many decades, they were able to establish the import of those pearls into India.

Non-nucleated Pearls

Non-nucleated pearls are formed in either salt water or fresh water when the oyster rejects and spits out the implanted nucleus before the culturing process is complete. Keshi pearls may form when the remaining pearl sacs produce pearls without a nucleus; these are generally small in size. Keshi pearls are composed entirely of nacre and tend to have a high lustre as a result; they are non-nucleated cultured pearls that occur in a variety of shapes, sizes and colours. The term keshi was first used in Japan during the late nineteenth and early twentieth centuries to describe natural seed pearls without a nucleus. When the Japanese began to cultivate Akoya pearls (created by a pearl farmer under controlled conditions), the name keshi was given to the by-products that were created after rejection of a bead nucleus. South Sea keshi pearls are generally larger than Japanese Akoya keshi pearls. In the late nineteenth/early twentieth centuries, when the Japanese Akoya pearl industry was at its peak, they provided numerous small keshi pearls, as by-products, to the international market.

The Hope Pearl
© Natural History Museum, London

François Flameng (1856–1923)
Portrait of Zinaida Yusupova wearing
the La Pelegrina pearl. 1894.
Oil on Canvas
© The State Hermitage Museum, St Petersburg

Historical Pearls

Hope Pearl

At the beginning of the nineteenth century, Henry Philip Hope acquired a large (1,800 grain, 450 carat or 90 gramme), natural, saltwater, pear-shaped baroque pearl of Oriental origin; it was 5.08 cm in length, with a circumference of 11.43 cm at its broadest point. It came to be known as the Hope Pearl. According to ancient tradition, the pearl was mounted as a pendant attached to a diamond-set ring and capped with a red-enamelled arched crown also set with diamonds, rubies and emeralds. It is not entirely clear which heir left the Hope Pearl to the South Kensington Museum (later the Victoria and Albert Museum) after Henry Hope's death. In 1886, the Hope Pearl was purchased at auction by Messrs Garrad & Co. of London. Then, in 1975, the Hope Pearl was purchased again by H. E. Mohammed Mahdi Al-Tajir, ambassador of the United Arab Emirates to Great Britain and to France. It appears that the ambassador sold the Hope Pearl to an anonymous private collector from England, who has loaned the Hope Pearl to the Natural History Museum, London, where it is on display.

La Pelegrina

The original weight of the perfect pear-shaped pearl is 133.16 grains. Little is known about the pearl's origin, but it is believed to have come from the coast of the isle of Santa Margarita in the Gulf of Panama during the mid-sixteenth century. The pearl made its first appearance in Spain in 1660. It arrived in France via royal alliances and was later sold to the Russian nobles of the House of Yusupov. A portrait of the Russian Zinaida Yusupova shows her wearing the pearl. During the October Revolution of 1917 many jewels from the Yusupov collection were taken by the Bolsheviks, but Zinaida's son Felix Yusupova managed to smuggle La Pelegrina out of Russia. History tells us that the pearl was sold in 1953 to Jean Lombard, a jeweller in Geneva. In May 1987 the pearl was again sold at auction in Geneva.

1. Tank, *Indian Gemmology.*

2. Foster, *The Embassy of Sir Thomas Roe to India* 1615 – 1619, pp.450, 457, 458.

Gold *guttapusal,* necklace
Andhra Pradesh, probably Hyderabad
Late eighteenth century

weight: 363 g
length: 58 cm

Elaborate gold *guttapusal* necklace, made up of a series of
eighty-three open double-tube-shaped elements, each set with
a cabochon ruby or emerald and a pearl on top, alternated on
either side with seven petal-shaped decorations each set with
a single diamond, ruby or emerald. On either side of the centre
pendant is an oval-shaped element attached to the double-tube-
shaped pendant each set with a single diamond bordered with
cabochon rubies and crowned with three pearls. Suspended from
it, a petal-shaped pendant set with a cabochon ruby and irregular
pearls. Three floret decorations are attached to the pendants
on either side of the oval-shaped elements. The largest pendant
at the centre has four cabochon rubies and four diamonds set
around a centre diamond and also crowned with three pearls.
Suspended from it is a single diamond and irregular pearls. All
pendants have irregular pearls hanging in clusters on gold wire.

All double-tube-shaped elements are strung on a loop-in-loop
gold wire necklace with a triangle-shaped gold screw-post clasp.

*On the south-east of the subcontinent, the Coromandel Coast was famous
for pearl fishery where, in its heyday, thousands of people were employed
during the pearl-diving season and behind almost every door were pearl
sorters, drillers and stringers. Hyderabad was historically known as the City
of Pearls. Long before this, pearl dust was popular among Hyderabadis as a
medicine known as* moti podi.

Further information:
Bala Krishnan and Kumar, *Indian Jewellery,* p.94
Carvalho, Sharp and Vernoit, *Gems and Jewels of Mughal India,* pp.196, 197
Van Gelder, *The Origin of Quality,* p.17

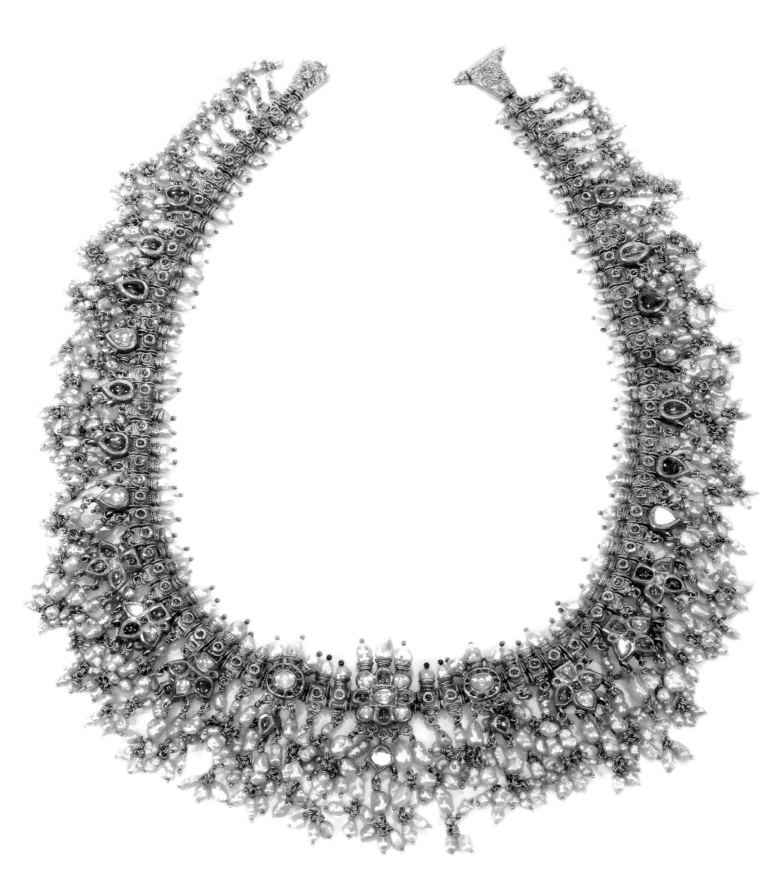

Set of four gold bangles
Rajasthan, Bikaner
Early nineteenth century

Set of four delicate gold bangles. The outer surface of each bangle is decorated with *kundan*-set, rose-cut, *polki* diamonds surrounded by pearls. The flat inner faces are of an opaque white enamel with red-enamelled flowers and green-enamelled leaves; the outer rim and hinges show traces of powder-blue enamel. The two parts are joined by an anti-clockwise screw.

Bali, nose ring
Western Rajasthan, Barmer district
Early twentieth century

Elaborate gold *bali or balu* nose ring with its original chain, which
is hooked onto the hair or head cloth. The *bali* is decorated with
different colours of irregular tourmaline beads, pearls and gold
beads. This style reflects the early jewellery design of the Bukhara
region in Uzbekistan.

Further information:
Hasson, *Later Islamic Jewellery*, p.107, illustration 147

Gold *timaniyaan*, necklace
Bikaner
Nineteenth century

Gold *timaniyaan*, wedding necklace, set with white sapphires
and suspended tassels of pearls and ruby beads. The necklace
ornament is suspended from multiple strands of seed pearls.

*A Rajasthani bride is adorned with lots of jewellery on her wedding day and
usually wears a red bridal saree, ghagra choli; symbolising prosperity and
fertility; red is an auspicious colour for brides. The bridal jewellery consists of: a
gold* aad, tevta *or* timaniyaan *(choker around the neck);* mangalsutra *(beaded
necklace);* matapatti *(gold ornament worn along the parting of the hair);* nath
(nose ring); several gold ear ornaments; chuda *(wide bangles);* paunchi *and*
haath phul *(a decoration for the hand, ankle and wrist);* baju *(armlets for the
upper arm);* pajeb *(jewellery for the ankle); and* bicchiya *(toe ring with little
bells, worn on the three middle toes).*

Further information:
Babur's Heritage, p.84

Ear pendants
Karnataka
Early twentieth century

Gold ear pendants decorated with pearls and a large coral bead.

Gold *jhumar*
North India
Nineteenth century

length: 9 cm
height, upper part: 3 cm
width, upper part: 4 cm
weight: 85 g

Elaborate double-sided headdress with a gold top and lower part
kundan-set with diamonds and cabochon rubies. The other side
is *kundan*-set with cabochon emeralds and pearls. The two gold
sections are connected by eleven strings of pearls alternated with
emerald beads. Attached on top is a double pearl and emerald
string for fastening in the hair.

Further information:
Hendley, *Indian Jewellery*, plate 5, illustration 22
Untracht, *Traditional Jewelry of India*, p.216, illustration 424
Stronge, Smith and Harle, *A Golden Treasury*, p.58

Oval miniature portrait painting
North India
Nineteenth century

Gold-mounted miniature painting on ivory, depicting an Indian
lady wearing gold jewellery in the Muslim tradition, including a
jhumar (pearl head ornament worn on the forehead). In front
of her ear she wears the *kanotti machchli,* a fish-shaped pendant
suspended from strings of pearls. Behind the *kanotti machchli* she
wears a *karanphul jhumka* (a flower-like ear stud) with a bell-
shaped lower part. Around her neck is a long double-row pearl
necklace and several short necklaces.

Further information:
Babur's Heritage

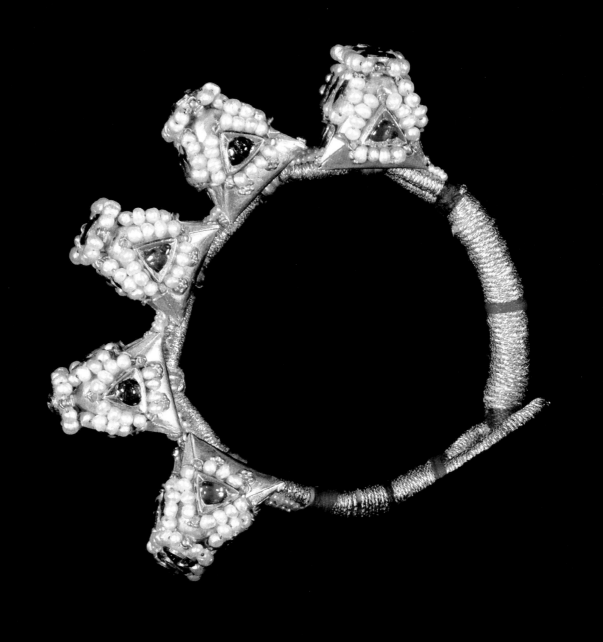

Pair of bracelets
Rajasthan, Ajmer region
Nineteenth century

weight: 224 g
length: 12 cm

A pair of bracelets featuring five gold ornaments strung with seed
pearls in a *gajra* pattern and *kundan*-set with cabochon emeralds,
rubies and a white sapphire in the centre. The five ornaments are
strung on a double row of seed pearls. The bracelet closes with a
loop and a rosette-shaped button.

Necklace with seven *tawiz* pendants
Uttar Pradesh, Lucknow
The *tawiz* are late eighteenth century
The pearl work is early twentieth century

Pearl necklace with seven container-shaped *tawiz* pendants, decorated with *lal zamin* (red enamel) and set with diamonds. Two of the *tawiz* have *makara*-head finials.

This type of pearl work is called *gajra*, meaning flowers tied together to form a garland.

The two *makara* heads are decorated with red and blue enamel on a gold ground, the eyes are two cat's eyes, the sharp teeth are gold with a white- and blue-enamelled rim on the curling snout, the tongue is a red garnet, there are some traces of green enamel inside the ears.

In Hindu mythology, the makara *is a sea-creature and the* vahana *(vehicle) of the goddess Ganga, the river goddess and the sea god Varuna. It is also the insignia of Kamadeva, the god of love. The* makara *is the astrological sign of Capricorn, one of the twelve symbols of the zodiac. Like other fabulous monsters, the* makara *is a mixture of several creatures.*

Guluband or *thussi*, necklace
Rajasthan, Bikaner
Nineteenth century

weight: 299 g
length: 25.5 cm
height: 3.5 cm

Gold *guluband* or *thussi*, worn high around the neck, consisting of
decorated chevron-shaped hollow segments with two loops on
top and suspended small gold beads. The necklace is embellished
on either side with peacock-shaped ornaments, four circular
floral designs, two oblong designs and in the centre a crescent
and sun theme. All *kundan*-set with cabochon Burmese rubies,
Colombian emeralds and white sapphires. The circular ornaments
are bordered with pearls.

Gajredar or *naugari,* pair of bracelets
Rajasthan, Shekavati Region
Early nineteenth century

Pair of pearl and gold bracelets, formed by five half-cylindrical units covered with a closely set cluster of pearls (*moti jali*). The centre is decorated with a rosette of *kundan*-set white sapphires. The units are attached by gold wire to gold 'saucers', which are polychrome enamelled at the bottom with a flower-and-bird motif and fastened to a double row of cords ending in a button-and-loop fastening.

Further information:
Babur's Heritage, p.84
Aitken, *When Gold Blossoms,* p.118, illustration 124

Gold necklace
Madhya Pradesh, Indore
Late eighteenth century

Gold necklace set with cabochon rubies and emeralds in zig-zag-aligned segments, crowned with pearls and decorated with suspended bunches of pearls and tiny gold beads. The gold segments and pearls are attached to the original *passementrie* of gold and silver wire, so-called *ruperi zari,* thread embroidery.

The joined W-shapes create a zig-zag pattern, which suggests flowing water, a symbol of fertility.

Gold 'sea creature' pendant with large natural baroque pearl
Europe
Early nineteenth century

weight: 42 g
width: 5.5 cm

Rare gold pendant, shaped in the form of a *makara* (a mythical aquatic beast), with a body consisting of an exceptionally large saltwater natural baroque pearl. The head shows powder blue and black enamel, the eyes are cabochon rubies. The back part of the body is set with four cabochon emeralds, a red- and white-enamelled tail with white-, green- and turquoise-enamelled dots. Two gold chains with four red enamel links hold the pendant, the chains are joined at the top by a gold-, red- and blue-enamelled roundel which is set on both sides with a cabochon emerald. Two irregular pearls are suspended from the roundel.

The reverse shows the scaled body with traces of green and red enamel, the powder-blue and white fins have small, gold enamel dots. The belly has several touches of red, green, white and turquoise enamel and is set with three cabochon emeralds. The jaw shows white enamel paint in the form of waves and white-enamelled teeth and the powder-blue enamel on the left and right indicates the gill-arch. The tail is red-enamelled with white-, turquoise- and green-enamelled touches.

Since aquatic beasts play an important role in Indian mythology and art, the Indian river crocodile Gavialis gangeticus, called the gharias or makara (Sanskrit), with the head of a crocodile and the body and tail of a fish, is one of the most indigenous among these fabulous Indian mythical creatures. It goes back more than two thousand years to a time when the natural world was seen as both symbol and reality and fantastic creatures were invented to express the complexity of nature. The makara has magical and occult powers and the motif has adorned the headdresses, earrings, armbands and hip belts of countless Hindu gods and has decorated the columns, brackets, lintels and ceilings of the temples that house them. Traditionally, festoons and strings of pearls poured forth from the gaping mouth of this monster of the primeval waters, symbolising the abundance of the sea. The makara is the symbol of the fertility of rivers, lakes and the sea, which consequently represents the essence of life. The makara also symbolises happiness and is an auspicious sign; it is the vehicle of Varuna, god of the waters of Heaven and Earth. The makara is also the vahana ('vehicle') of the goddess Ganga, the personification of the sacred river Ganges. It is the emblem of Kama the god of love and desire. Sometimes, makara is referred to as a seizure that snares or entraps its victim; it was an act of proverbial courage to extract a pearl from a makara's mouth.

The massive natural baroque pearl with its lustrous sheen comes from the Pinctada maxima oyster and came historically from the Pacific Ocean near the coasts of Malaysia, Mergui Archipelago (Burma), Sulu Archipelagos (Philippines) and North-West Australia. For nearly four hundred years, these large pearls were traded to India, the Middle East and, since the discovery of the sea route by Vasco da Gama in 1498, also to Europe where, during the Renaissance, the baroque pearl became much sought after. Renaissance jewellery-makers came under Indian influence and the result is a hybrid of subjects, symbols and materials.

The basic shapes of these large baroque pearls inspired craftsmen from northern Italy and southern Germany to create splendid jewelled objects in combination with precious stones and, often, enamel. Pendants in the form of large fish, tritons and nereids were favourite subjects. They were often displayed with a body created from a large baroque pearl so as to confirm the bond with the sea and therefore often used as talismans for seafarers.

Renaissance designs created a spirit of retrospection in the arts during the nineteenth century and two major jewellery styles emerged: Gothic, or Medieval, and Renaissance Revival. The pendant here shows a typical design of European nineteenth-century revival with a typical Indian theme, which makes the jewel quite interesting and rare. The influence of India, however, is quite pronounced in Guiliano's jewellery. Widespread interest in Indian art was a result of nineteenth century British imperialism and the enormous amount of trade generated in the East. The Guiliano bequest of 1895 to the South Kensington Museum contained an ornate pendant of multicoloured champlevé enamels, which was said to be 'an imitation 'of the enamelled work of Jaipur and a wide range of jewellery reflected the theme. Important examples of baroque pearl use in Renaissance jewellery can be found in museum collections all over the world. Several examples featured in Renaissance Jewellery by Yvonne Hackenbroch show a striking similarity with the makara pendant mentioned above.*

* Munn, *Castellani and Guiliano, Revivalist Jewellers of the Nineteenth Century*, p.129.

Further information:
Hackenbroch, *Renaissance Jewellery*, p.326, image 866. It is interesting to note that the 'Indians riding the sea creature' are, in fact, indigenous peoples of the Americas (p.327, images 871, 872, 873) so not related to the subcontinent.

Diamonds

The Lure of Vajra

'The diamond of the Brahmin should have the whiteness of a shell or of rock-crystal; that of the Kshatriya, the brown colour of the eye of a hare; that of the Vaisya, the lovely shade of a petal of the kadali flower; that of the Sudra, the sheen of a polished blade.'

In Indian mythology, diamond is referred to as *vajra* (meaning 'thunderbolt'), hence it is the magical weapon of Indra, god of the heavens and the chief deity of the Rigvedic pantheon. In ancient Sanskrit texts, diamond is referred to as *hira* or *hiraka* (the jewel above all others).

According to the earliest historical records, rough diamonds date back some 3,000 years, and India was one of the earliest countries to mine the mineral.

The history of diamonds is one of mystical power and myths about valleys in India hosting diamonds protected against intruders by snakes. As a protector and benefactor, diamond had no equal and was at the forefront of ancient Indian desire. It had ornamental and artistic value as well as being used as a talisman to ward off evil or provide protection in the battlefield. It was believed that the talismanic power of the diamond only became active when it was received as a gift and not if it was acquired as a purchase.

George Frederick Kunz writes in his preface to *The Curious Lore of Precious Stones*:

'all the fair colours of flowers and foliage and even the blue of the sky and the glory of the sunset clouds only last for a short time and are subject to continual changes but the sheen and colouration of precious stones are the same today as they were thousands of years ago and will be for thousands of years to come.'

Sarpech, turban ornament
Andhra Pradesh, Hyderabad
Late nineteenth century

height: 9 cm
width: 5.5 cm
weight: 53 g

Silver turban ornament set with irregular-shaped flat-cut diamonds on foil and decorated with seven diamond-set pendants, each with three pearls. The lower part is set with a greenish cat's eye.

Diamond derives its name from the Latin *adamantis* and the Greek *adamas*. It is the toughest natural gemstone known to mankind, with crystals made up entirely of carbon. Diamonds possess an unsurpassed hardness of 10 on the Mohs scale.[1] The gem quality is such that it is among the earth's most valuable treasures, prized by emperors and conquerors throughout history.

Many of the great diamonds of the world, some of which are found today in the collections of royalty and in crown jewels, have their association with central South India, the region of Rayalaseema in the state of Andhra Pradesh, where some thirty-eight mines existed during the sixteenth, seventeenth and eighteenth centuries.

To this day, diamonds in India are stones of destiny, cherished because of their brilliant purity and flashes of fire, their spiritual value, their symbolic position in the zodiac and their role in astrology. They represent the powerful aura of the cosmos and its connection with mankind.

Hindus have their Panchratna (five gems) usually consisting of diamond, ruby, sapphire, emerald and pearl. Within the traditional *nava ratna* arrangement (a specific combination of nine gems), *vajra* (diamond) is associated with the supernatural energies of Shukra (Venus). Diamonds were transformed into elaborate offerings for the gods and presented in temples.

Diamonds are grouped by colour and quality according to the four *varnas*, the social system within Hinduism. George Frederick Kunz in *The Curious Lore of Precious Stones* (p.73) writes:

'The ancient Hindu gem-treatise of Buddhabhatta asserts that
the diamond of the Brahmin should have the whiteness of a shell or of rock-crystal;
that of the Kshatriya, the brown colour of the eye of a hare;
that of the Vaisya, the lovely shade of a petal of the kadali flower;
that of the Sudra, the sheen of a polished blade.'

Diamond Trade

History shows that there was already a diamond trade in the third century BC between the Red Sea and the Persian Gulf, and the most important ports on the Mediterranean and around the Black Sea.

Until the late 1400s, the only route from India to Europe was overland through Persia, traversing the ancient Silk Road caravan routes across the Chinese–Indian subcontinent, Persia, Arabia and Europe. This was a dangerous and costly journey and there was a significant risk that large quantities of diamonds would fall into Persian hands as a 'protection for crossing their territory'.

From the early sixteenth century, with the establishment of the direct sea route between Portugal and India by the Portuguese admiral Vasco da Gama, the diamond trade took off. From India's Malabar coast all the way to Lisbon (Portugal), and later, under the control of the export market by the Dutch East India Company, up to

Map of India showing Tavernier's routes and the sites of the diamond mines mentioned by him, from *Travels in India*, Volume 1 by Jean Baptiste Tavernier

the north of Europe, where Antwerp and Amsterdam rose to become the world's premier centres for cutting as well as polishing rough diamonds.

Velha Goa (Old Goa) soon became the greatest trading area in Asia for all kinds of luxury goods such as silk, textiles, precious stones and pearls.

Bhagnagar was the name of the capital of the Kingdom of Golconda (also known simply as Golconda), taken from the name of the fortress nearby where the king resided. The fortress, first built on a granite hill, but expanded through time, rose to prominence as the seat of the Qutb Shahi Dynasty until 1590, when the capital was shifted to Hyderabad. The best quality diamonds from Rayalaseema region were mined during the Qutb Shahi Dynasty and many tons were moved into the Kingdom of Golconda.

It was a rich kingdom, abounding in corn, rice, cattle, sheep, fowl and other commodities necessary for survival, but the region became best known for the group of mines concentrated around the Krishna or Kistná river. Large diamonds were found there, predominantly in the alluvial deposits of the river.

History tells us that one of the first travellers to the area in the Deccan Plateau was the Flemish jewel trader Jacques de Coutre in 1612. He visited the mine of Ramallakota; followed by a group of three European merchants led by the English William Methwold, a servant of the English East India Company at Masulipatam and Governor of Surat, who visited the Kingdom of Golconda between 1618 and 1622.

Jean Baptiste Tavernier (1605–1689) the seventeenth-century French connoisseur of gems, merchant and traveller, made six travels to the East over a period of almost forty years (1630–1668). Five of his voyages brought him to the subcontinent and four included trips to the mines near Golconda, noting many details of the Indian gem trade. While trading constantly, en route to India and returning, he saved its best gemstones for France and King Louis XIV, who in gratitude granted him the title of Baron. In 1669 he purchased the Seigneury of Aubonne in the vicinity of Genève and became Baron of Aubonne.

Tavernier mentioned that on all purchases made, two per cent of the value had to be paid to the King of Golconda, who not only owned the mine, but also received royalties from the entrepreneur in return for permission to mine.

Tavernier visited the Kingdom of Golconda for the first time during his voyage between 1638 and 1643, and became a very important contact for the trade between India and Europe. Thus he became known as the Father of the Diamond Trade.

According to Tavernier there were twenty-three mines over a vast area on the eastern side of the Deccan Plateau and most of the mines were within the territory of the old Kingdom of Golconda. It was here that the most fabled and largest diamonds were unearthed. Tavernier also mentioned fifteen mines in the neighbouring Kingdom of Bijapur.

His surviving travel journals (*Travels in India* in two volumes) give us a fairly accurate account of diamonds in India at the peak period of their discovery and supply to the world.[2]

The journals also provided detailed historic records about Indian life and the huge wealth at the Mughal Courts.

Until the early eighteenth century, when diamonds were discovered in South America (Minas Gerais, Brasil, 1725), India was the only diamond supplier for the entire world.

Mining

Different regions had different methods of excavating the mineral. It all depended on how close the diamond-bearing deposits were to the surface. In some areas it was necessary to mine at great depth, but in Kondapettah deposits were found less than four feet below the surface, from where it was possible to retrieve the gravel and have it washed, dried and examined in order to select the particles that were sparkling bright and clear.

For a long time, the local rulers kept the finding places secret. In the course of the sixteenth century more foreign merchants and adventurers were attracted to the areas and the fabled mines of the Kingdom of Golconda became the key places for finding diamonds of spectacular size and of the best quality. Soon the fortress city within the walls became the trading centre for the entire region.

In the bazaars, the trade from around twenty-one mines across the Kingdom of Golconda was dazzling and mind blowing. The highest quality stones of unimaginable richness from the mines in Ramallakota, Partiyala, Kulur and Kondapettah were found by collectors, but royalty and the wealthy nobility reserved the right to keep the highest quality and largest stones for themselves.

No stone over five carats in weight could be sold, as it was regarded as the property of royalty. Diamonds not retrained by the court were sold at official auctions.

From early accounts we know of Marco Polo's travels (1292) from China through India back home to Italy: no other country than the Kingdom of Mutfili (later Golconda) produced diamonds, but there they were found both abundantly and of large size. Those that were brought to Europe were the rejects. The choicest diamonds and other large gems, as well as larger pearls, were all carried to the Great Khan and other kings and princes from those regions; in truth they possessed all the great treasures of the world.[3]

It was recorded that at the height of production around 60,000 people worked and mined the region, including women and children.

Although the sites where carefully watched by guards, miners created ingenious ways to smuggle stones out. Once a diamond had been smuggled away from the mines, its possessor was not only safe, but if it was of large size, and he offered it to either the King of Golconda or the King of Bijapur, he had every chance of selling it well, and being presented with a robe of honour.[4]

The Kulur, or Kollur, mine in the Guntur district of old Golconda, approximately eighty kilometres from the Bay of Bengal, on the right bank of the river Krishna, was the largest and the most productive. Diamonds of between 10 and 40 carats were found in the Kulur mine.

Tavernier writes: 'the largest and most perfect of the diamonds from Kulur were presented to the Emperor. Among them the uncut "Great Mogul" diamond, which was presented to Emperor Shah Jahan in the year 1656–1657 by Mir Jumla, a reputed diamond dealer from Persia, who had risen to the position of Vizier of the Kingdom of Golconda.'

The weight of the then largest existing stone was, according to Tavernier, 900 rattis (one ratti equals approximately 1.125 carats) or 787.5 (English) carats. Some years later (1665) Tavernier mentioned the diamond again but it was then in the treasury of Emperor Aurengzeb.

It has been recorded that, unfortunately, the beautiful stone was downsized to 319.5 rattis, or 279.563 carats, due to wasteful grinding instead of cleaving, by Hortensio Borgio from Venice, Italy.[5]

In Golconda the size of a diamond was estimated by its weight in *manjali,* which is a seed weighing approximately the equivalent of four or five troy grains, and equals about 1.333 carats.

In the early eighteenth century, ca. 1725, diamonds were discovered in Brazil, and India was no longer the only source of rough diamonds. Because of intensive mining, the famous mines became depleted and Golconda turned into a deplorable site.

Diamond cutters at work

Then, one and a half centuries later, ca. 1886, diamonds were also discovered in South Africa. This left the once so famous mining area behind.

Today the diamond industry in India focuses on cutting and polishing, and is concentrated in Surat, in the State of Gujarat, and Mumbai. There are some 13,000 companies in Gujarat involved in diamond cutting and polishing, of which Surat has about 10,000 diamond units.

Throughout history, the term 'Golconda diamond' has been, and is still, used as a generic term for top-quality diamonds mined in India.

Cut Forms, Settings and Colour

In the beginning no effort was made to give the stones any form, because of the fear of reducing the weight. When the natural crystal was so perfect and clear that it required only to have its natural facets polished, then it was preferable that it was used as a large pendant or talisman. Cleavability of diamonds was known to Indian lapidaries at the time of Tavernier's visits to India, even the knowledge that two diamonds rubbed together ground each other was applied.

Up to the early fifteenth century the only patterns known were fairly basic such as *polki,* flat- and point-cut. Much later the rose cut was introduced with a flat base and dome-shaped top and triangular facets.

Over a period of time, diamonds, along with other gemstones, developed different cuts, ranging from the simplest cut (referred to as the 'Indian cut') to the most intricate engraving with flora, fauna and Islamic motifs. The tradition was for a closed setting with shiny and coloured foil underneath, to create even more brilliance.

Diamonds vary from colourless to very dark, almost black, and may be transparent, translucent or opaque. Gem-quality diamonds are colourless and 'whiter than white' as old Golconda diamonds show.

Diamonds used in old *kundan*-set jewellery have different forms and cuts:

Polki, with one side flat and the other sides faceted to a taper, resembling a rose cut, which it is not. However, several types of rose-cut diamond may appear in traditional Indian jewellery, rose-cut with three, six, eight or more facets. *Parab*, with a smaller taper and more facets then *polki*. *Mukalasi* is faceted on both sides. *Villandi* is where the upper part is flat, the lower part which is mounted uppermost, is irregularly faceted to a vertex. Mughal-cut refers to stones which, after being cut, keep the maximum weight of the original rough stone.

Then there is the rough, uncut diamond, the *karakht*, when the stone was of such an exceptional size and quality that it could have been inscribed with the name and dates of its owner, as is the case with the famous Shah Diamond.

The Indian term for the Western channel setting is *talpain*. Also used for square or rectangular rubies or emeralds set with no metal shown between the stones. The more recent *kanwal* cut is referred to as the 'brilliant cut' in the West. This cut adds more facets to the stone to give the diamond more lustre.

For coloured gemstones the *pota* or cabochon cut is used, with a dome-shaped top and flat bottom. Loose beads may be carved in a melon shape, known as *kharbuja manovatdar*. *Kharbuja* means 'melon' and *manovatdar* means 'carving'.

Famous Diamonds

Koh-I-Noor, 'Mountain of Light'

Writers and historians on this subject are numerous, so are the facts and approximations to the weight of this gem.

Nadir Shah (Shah of Persia, 1698–1747) invaded India and sacked Delhi in 1739. Among the trove of fabulous jewels were the Takht-I Tawus (or 'Peacock Throne') and the Koh-I-Noor ('Mountain of Light'), first named by Nadir Shah.

The Koh-i-nûr armlet ca.1830
Gold, enamel, rock crystal, glass, rubies, pearls and silk
Royal Collection Trust/© Her Majesty Queen Elizabeth II 2017

From then on the Koh-I-Noor travelled through history from the Deccan Plateau to Delhi to Iran and later came into the possession of the Sikh Ruler of the Punjab, Ranjit Singh, known as the Lion of Punjab, where it remained until 1849. He had the stone mounted with two other stones on each side in a gold-enamelled armlet (*bazuband*).

After the British annexation of the Punjab, the Koh-I-Noor became the property of the East India Company. In 1850 the Koh-i-Noor left India to sail to Britain on board HMS *Medea* and has never returned. It was presented by Sir John Lawrence, a British Imperial statesman, on 3 July 1850 to Queen Victoria. It subsequently became a major attraction when on display during the Great Exhibition at the Crystal Palace in London, 1851. In 1854 its former owner, the twelve-year-old Maharaja Dalip Singh (1838–1893) travelled to Great Brittain.

Queen Victoria bequeathed the stone to Queen Alexandra, her daughter-in-law and wife of King Edward VII, Emperor of India. During her coronation as Queen of Great Britain and Empress of India, in 1902, she wore the Imperial Crown, which contained the Koh-I-Noor. It was later set as the centrepiece in the State Crown of Queen Mary (1911), and later still, transferred to the State Crown of King George VI's wife, Queen Elizabeth (1937). To this day the Koh-I-Noor rests in the Jewel House at the Tower of London among the Crown Jewels.

The earlier history of the gem is hidden in the mists of time and legends linked with the authentic history take us back to the dawn of the fourteenth century (1304) when the stone was reported to be in the ownership of Mahlak Deo, the Rajah of Malwa.

More than two centuries later, when Babur came to Agra in 1526, the famous diamond was mostly tendered to him, according to the records in the Babur Nama, the memoirs of the first Mughal Emperor Babur, since which time it was referred to as 'Babur's Diamond', weighing about 320 rattis, equivalent to about 186 or 187 (English) carats according to Professor Maskelyne (1732–1811) and V. Ball at the time. There is strong evidence to suggest that Babur handed over the diamond to his son Humayun.

Another early mention in the history of the stone is an account by the traveller and physician François Bernier. In his *Travels in the Moghul Empire 1656–1668* he mentioned the stone when Mir Jumla presented the gem, 'unparalleled in size and beauty' to Emperor Shah Jahan, advising him to despatch an army for the conquest of Golconda.

Over the course of the next two centuries the fabulous gem was passed on to successive generations of rulers and finally came into the possession of Emperor Muhammad Shah (reign 1719–1748). At that time the Mughal empire had been weakened by a ruinous war of succession lasting three decades, which brought the Persian ruler Nadir Shah, attracted by the country's wealth, victory over the Mughals after the battle of Karnal in 1738. He sacked Delhi in 1739 and forced Emperor Muhammad Shah to hand over the royal treasury, including the fabulous Peacock Throne. Nadir Shah also gained the Koh-I-Noor and a second great diamond called the Darya-I-Noor, respectively 'Mountain of Light' and 'Sea of Light'.

After the assassination of Nadir Shah (1747) the Koh-I-Noor changed hands again until it reached its new owner, the Maharaja Ranjit Singh, ruler of the Sikh empire in the Punjab. On 29 March 1849, the Kingdom of Punjab was formally annexed to British India and the Koh-i-Noor became the brightest jewel in the British Crown.

It will be convenient to mention that in 1889, Mr V. Ball, translator of *Travels in India* by Jean Baptiste Tavernier, mentioned in Appendix I, p.431, that principal authorities had different theories concerning the Koh-i-Noor:

1. Those who equate the identity of the Koh-i-Noor with Babur's Diamond.
2. Those who equate the identity of the Koh-i-Noor with the Great Mogul and who either treat Babur's Diamond as distinct or make no special reference to it.
3. Those who equate the identity of the Koh-i-Noor with both Babur's Diamond and the Great Mogul.

The Great Mogul

In Tavernier's travel journals there is also mention of a few other remarkable stones, among them a round rose-cut diamond, presented in the form of an egg cut in half, which he claimed to have seen in the treasury at the court of the Great Moghul Aurengzeb in 1665. It was named The Great Mogul, unearthed in the Kollur mine in the vicinity of Golconda around 1650 during the reign of Emperor Shah Jahan. The diamond, which in its rough state once weighed 787.50 carats according to Tavernier, was later recorded as the largest of the great diamonds in India, that is according to the accepted accounts of its ambiguous history.

Tavernier referred to it in his *Travels in India*, Volume II, claiming the Venetian lapidary named Hortensio Borgio had reduced the weight of this diamond to about 280 carats! Some scholars and historians suggest that the story of the diamond's cutting by Borgio is doubtful, because at that time, according to the Indian historian N. B. Sen[6] local Indian cutters were considered to be more experienced and skillful than Western craftsmen. So the question arises: would Aurengzeb have assigned the task to a Venetian cutter, and why is such a historic blunder not noticed in the records kept by Aurengzeb's chroniclers? Furthermore, over time, the Great Mogul and the Orlov have been compared and the similarity in shape between Tavernier's drawing of the Great Mogul and the images of the Orlov is perfectly clear; also the Orlov has been independently described as resembling half a 'pigeon's egg'.

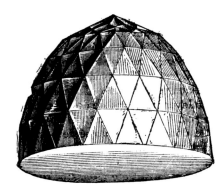

The Great Mogul
© morphart/123RF Stock Photo

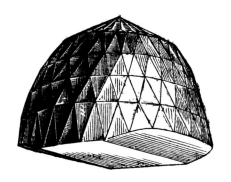

Orlov
© morphart/123RF Stock Photo

Orlov

The rose-cut Orlov diamond, is one of the most important gems in one of the world's greatest collections of gems and jewellery, the Treasures of the Diamond Fund, Gokran. The Orlov, mounted in the Imperial Sceptre beneath the golden eagle, is displayed in the Kremlin Museum in Moscow. Its weight has been recorded as 189.62 carats and it measures 47.6 mm in height, 31.75 mm in width and 34.92 mm in length.

According to an early account, the gem was the eye of an idol in Ranganathaswamy Temple located in Srirangam, Tamil Nadu. It is one of the most illustrious Vaishnava temples in South India. It was a French grenadier, as the story goes, who stole one of the precious 'eyes' of the idol and sold it in Madras to an English sea captain who carried the stone to London. After passing through several hands it came into the possession of an Armenian merchant called Grigori Safras who had moved to Amsterdam.

In 1774 Count Grigory Grigoryevich Orlov of Russia (1734–1783) acquired the diamond in Amsterdam (from Safras), and it is known these days as the Amsterdam diamond. Count Orlov presented the diamond to Catherine II Empress of Russia (1729–1796) as proof of his love for her and to remind the empress of the role he had played in her accession to the throne. His reward was the honour of bestowing his name to the diamond and a marble palace at St Petersburg, but he was never again restored as her lover.

The Shah

The Shah, a peculiar bar-shaped Golconda diamond, not cut, with an original weight of 95 carats; after being partly polished its weight came to 88.7 carats.

Some important stones of gem quality were inscribed with the names of their imperial owners and passed down from one generation to the next; further names were added below those of the previous owners. One of the few known examples is the Shah Diamond, with three cleavage faces and inscribed on its three faces are the names of its three former owners. The three inscriptions give us evidence of the history of the Shah. The first date on the stone is the year 1000 in the Muslim calendar (corresponding to our year 1591) referring to Burhan Nizam Shah II, the ruler of the kingdom of Ahmadnagar, situated in north-west Deccan.

The second inscription reads 'Son of Jahangir, Shah Jahan, 1051' (corresponding to our calendar 1641).

The third inscription is that of the Persian ruler Fath Ali Shah (the ruler of Qajar, who inherited the diamond after Nadir Shah's sack of Delhi) and the year is 1824. The inscriptions testify to the diamond's history and provenance and make it one of the most important relics of Mughal India.

The diamond was presented to Tsar Nicholas I of Russia by Khusrau Mirza as compensation for the murder (in 1829) of Alexander Sergeyevich Griboyedov, who was appointed Minister of Persia. The diamond is to be found in the Russian Diamond Fund and is on display in The Kremlin in Moscow.

The Hope Diamond

In early 1668, Jean Baptiste Tavernier sold a magnificent rough sapphire-like dark-blue diamond to the French king Louis XIV. It is believed that the gem was unearthed from the Kulur mine and weighed approximately 112 Florentine carats, or 116.67 carats.

The king had the lustrous stone recut in a heart shape weighing 67.12 carats. The amazing, blue Hope was now known as the Blue Diamond of the Crown. In 1749 Louis XV gave his court jeweller André Jacquemin, the order to craft both the French Blue and the Côte de Bretagne (spinel) into a ceremonial jewel in the decoration of the Order of the Golden Fleece.

The French Blue became part of a loot during the French Revolution in 1792 and was considered to be lost. Two decades later an irregular blue diamond appeared in London and was bought by Henry Philip Hope of Hope & Co. Since then the diamond has been called the Hope, in spite of the fact that its owners kept changing. Some time later the Hope was presented on the market again and purchased by the Parisian diamond merchant, C. H. Rosenau who sold it to Pierre Cartier, who had the fabulous stone mounted in a diamond necklace. Pierre Cartier sold the jewel in Washington DC to Mrs Evalyn Walsh McLean. Two years later, following the death of Mrs McLean, the Hope was purchased in 1949 by Harry Winston. Its wanderings ended on 10 November 1958, when Harry Winston presented the Hope to the Smithsonian Institute in Washington DC.

Most of the famous diamonds, now in Royal Treasuries and museums, known by their names came from India. This includes the Darya-i-Noor (Sea of light), the Dresden Green, the Pitt-Regent and the Nizam (277 carats) just to mention a few.

In the past it has happened more than once that large diamonds were reduced by cleaving into two or more stones, sometimes for the purpose of destroying their identity in cases when the diamond had been stolen. Some historians claim that not only was the Great Mogul cut into pieces, of which the Koh-i-Noor is one, but also the famous Orlov. However, other scholars claim there is still no evidence.

Throughout history, experts and historians have researched the authenticity of these great diamonds. Differing opinions on important stones have crossed our path. The multitude of speculations is sometimes confusing and questions remain unanswered, but what endures is an endless fascination for these great marvels and their history of war, love and intrigue.

The Hope Diamond
©2017 National Museum of Natural History,
National Gem Collection, Smithsonian

1. The Mohs scale of mineral hardness, named after Friedrich Mohs (a German mineralogist) who, in 1812, invented a scale of hardness based on the ability of one mineral to scratch another. There are ten minerals in the Mohs Scale (from softest to hardest): talc, gypsum, calcite, fluorite, apatite, feldspar, quartz, topaz, corundum and diamond.

2. Tavernier, *Travels in India*.

3. *Travels by Marco Polo* or *Il Millone* written down by Rustichello da Pisa.

4. Tavernier, *Travels in India*, Vol.II, p.59, footnote 2.

5. The Indian author N. B. Sen in his book *Glorious History of Koh-i-noor, the Brightest Jewel in the British Crown*.

Gold *bazuband*
North India
Nineteenth century

weight: 370 g
length: 19.5 cm
width: 7 cm

Gold *bazuband* (flexible armlet for the upper arm) with thirty-five interlocking vertical bars, each set with diamonds. The semicircular ends are set with larger diamonds in a floral pattern. Each vertical unit ends in a loop set with a diamond and two emeralds; cord is threaded through and tied to the upper arm. The cord ends in an elaborate tassel of gold and silver threads (*zari* work) with pearls and glass beads.

These type of *bazuband* are worn above the elbow.

The tradition of wearing this type of bracelet was inherited by the Mughals from their ancestors, the Timurids. The old traditional form was composed of a precious large stone, usually an emerald or spinel, flanked by two large pearls and tied around the upper arm. They became more ornate with time and were symbolic of

aristocracy and masculinity. Over the years they became more significant during provincial rule, when the Maharajas and other nobility would wear them to indicate their status.

Zari is a brocade of tinsel thread meant for weaving and embroidery and fabricated from fine gold or silver thread, which is flattened by passing it through rotating rollers exerting equal pressure. When *zari* is used for embroidery it is called *zardozi* or *karchobi* and was probably derived from the Persian word *zar*, meaning 'gold'. This style of embroidery was a result of the Mughal influence on Rajasthani courts and has survived through the ages.

The art of this age-old craft has been inherited by sons from their fathers for many centuries. It is recognised by the Indian government as one of the ancient handicrafts.

Diamond necklace
Lucknow
Early nineteenth century

Front
Important gold necklace of joined openworked segments in
the form of lotus flowers with a large rosette in the centre, all
kundan-set with irregular and flat-cut diamonds. The upper edge
is crowned with thirty-two small gold cups each holding a pearl.
A row of pearls is attached to the lower rim. Attached to the
necklace are drop-shaped pendants *kundan*-set with flat-cut
diamonds and gold wired pearls.

The openworked 'lotus' pattern gives a lace effect (*jali kam*).

Reverse
The reverse is densely enamelled in *champlevé* technique with
stylised flowers in red- and green-enamelled foliage on an
opaque white ground (*safed chalwan*).

Pair of gold and diamond ear pendants
Uttar Pradesh, Lucknow
Nineteenth century

length, total: 19 cm
weight: 82 g

Elaborate ear ornaments *kundan*-set with variously cut diamonds consisting of two parts.

The upper part is a peacock design decorated with a row of six pearls, an emerald bead hanging from its beak and a pearl on top of its head. Attached to the lower dome-shaped *jhumkhi* part are two rows of dangling pearls with blue glass beads and a single emerald bead hanging from the centre. A double gold chain is fixed at the top and supplied with a square diamond-set ornament and hook for attachment to the hair, helping to support its weight.

The reverse is polychrome enamelled in a floral pattern.

The peacock represents the very essence of Indian philosophy and occupies a respectable position in Indian culture. It is considered a symbol of love, grace and joy, and the richness of colours gives it a heavenly beauty. The peacock, known as mayura in Sanskrit, enjoys a fabled place in India, and is frequently depicted in temple art, mythology, poetry and traditions. Several Hindu deities are associated with the bird, for example, Kartikeya the god of war and general of the army of the gods, rides a peacock. Lord Krishna is often depicted with a peacock feather in his headdress.

Peacock motifs were widely used in jewellery designs, especially in ear ornaments in North India.

Gold triangle-shaped finials for a necklace
Hyderabad, Burhanpur
Early eighteenth century

width: 3.7 cm
height: 3 cm
weight, one triangle ornament: 24 g

The gold triangle-shaped ornaments are *kundan*-set with *polki* diamonds on a green-enamelled gold ground.

The *polki* cut is characterised by a flat tabletop and bottom and an arrangement of different-sized facets on the side. It is one of the most prevalent cuts for diamonds set in traditional Indian jewellery.

Reverse
The ornaments show a decoration of a flowering plant, chased and engraved, *champlevé*, with red, light-blue and green enamel on opaque white enamel.

Gold *tikka*, forehead ornament
Uttar Pradesh
Early nineteenth century

weight: 20 g
width: 2.8 cm
height: 3.5 cm

Gold *tikka* (forehead jewel) in the form of a crescent,
supporting a sun-shaped ornament, *kundan*-set with foiled
rose-cut *polki* diamonds, a cabochon ruby on top and ten
suspended pearls with a ruby bead in the centre.

Women wear the tikka *on their forehead, attached to a gold or pearl
chain, which is fastened into the hair.*

Gold *turrah*, turban ornament
North India, Delhi or Lahore
Eighteenth century

weight: 49 g
length : 9.5 cm
diameter, diamond-set rosette: 4 cm

Gold turban ornament, depicting a bird with a red-enamelled head and body. The bird is attached by two small gold loops and wire to a gently tapering pin with a decoration of green zig-zag and red dot enamel motifs. The *kundan*-set diamond wings are perched on top and a pearl is hanging from its beak; there is a further *kundan*-set diamond rosette with a screw at one side to hold the bird in place.

The double flower-head top piece is *kundan*-set with rose-cut diamonds and seven dangling pearls trimming the petals. At the reverse, the double flower-head top part is decorated with red enamel and inlaid with *kundan*-set diamonds. This top part can be unscrewed.

Further information:
A Kaleidoscope of Colours, p.54, exhibit number 06
Carvalho, Sharp and Vernoit, *Gems and Jewels of Mughal India*, pp.126, 127
Untracht, *Traditional Jewelry of India*, p.403, illustration 859

Pearl necklace with pendants
West Bengal, Kolkata

weight: 190 g
length: 38 cm

A traditional seven-strand pearl necklace (*sat lara har*); a gold openwork pendant set with diamonds and emeralds is attached at the centre of each strand. Tiny four-leaf-shaped pendants set with one small diamond in the centre and four small emeralds, are hanging from each pearl strand.

On either side the necklace shows two peacocks as gold triangular openwork terminals, set with diamonds, emeralds and two rubies.

The patua-style tying-on cord is traditional in India.

Ancient texts often mention long necklaces comprising a single strand or many. Since seven is an auspicious number, it is perhaps no surprise that seven-strand necklaces have been so popular.

Further information:
Untracht, *Traditional Jewelry of India*, p.374, photo 813
Van Campen and Hartkamp-Jonxis, *Asian Splendour*, p.85
Hendley, *Indian Jewellery*, plate 111, illustration 774

Gold *bale jhabbedar*, ear pendants
Uttar Pradesh and Punjab
Late nineteenth century

length: 9 cm
weight: 51 g

Elaborate pair of gold *bale jhabbedar* consisting of three parts.

The circular rosette is *kundan*-set with diamonds, decorated with
a rim of pearls and shows multicoloured enamel at the reverse.

Attached to the circular top are three petal-shaped pendants,
each set at the front and reverse with a diamond.

The larger petal-shaped centre part contains six smaller pendants.
On both sides it is set with carved green glass, decorated with a
diamond-set tree of life symbol.

The fish- and petal-shaped pendants are set on both sides with
diamonds, fringes of pearls and blue glass beads.

Further information:
Untracht, *Traditional Jewelry of India*, p.224, illustration 455

Gold diamond-set ring
Rajasthan, Bikaner
Nineteenth century

Gold rose-cut *polki* diamond ring, *kundan*-set with seven diamonds to form a rosette bordered with pearls; the band is decorated with multi-coloured enamel in a floral motif.

Originally, this ring was part of a haath phul *(hand flower) which is an elaborate jewel for the hand comprising four finger rings and an* arsi *(thumb ring) each linked by a chain to a centrepiece decorating the hand and is attached to a wristlet.*

Toti or *tops*, ear ornaments
Gujarat, Kutch
Eighteenth century

weight, pair: 100 g
diameter: 6 cm

A pair of gold ear ornaments, *toti* or *karnphul* (flower) with a gently convex-shaped front plate, *kundan*-set with an intricate design of a central diamond rosette surrounded by a radiating floral arrangement of irregular-sized *polki* or rose-cut diamonds and foiled cabochon emeralds.

Surrounding the central medallion are foiled channel or *talpain*-set rubies, interspersed with four foiled table-cut diamonds, bordered by a row of pearls. The outer edges are decorated with a rim of gold beads.

The reverse of each *toti* is plain gold and has a large plug at the back for the lobe. A screw with an attached back-plate keeps the ornament in place.

This type of ear ornament was originally worn only by men, nowadays they are worn by women as well and are also seen in silver, set with glass, rock crystal and other minerals on coloured foil.

Further information:
Ganguly, *Earrings, Ornamental Identity and Beauty in India*, p.93
Prior and Adamson, *Maharajas' Jewels*, p.21

Gold *guluband*, *arya* or *adyia*, neck ornament
Rajasthan, Bikaner
Nineteenth century

weight: 192 g
width of the rigid part: 12 cm
height: 9 cm

Gold and pearl-fringed *guluband*, *arya* or *adyia* (neck ornament). The rigid arched collar is decorated with an openwork foliate design with a sun and crescent jewel in the centre, and flanked by two peacocks. The *guluband* is *kundan*-set in the centre with a teardrop-shaped foiled flat-cut diamond, bordered by channel-set foiled emeralds. The crescent is also channel-set with seven oblong-shaped foiled diamonds in the *kundan* technique. To the left and right of the centre stone are cabochon emeralds. The other diamonds are *kundan*-set in the traditional geometric and organic shapes often seen in this type of jewellery. Eleven plain gold cups to which pearls are wired, decorate the upper edge of the *guluband*. Suspended from the rigid upper part are thirteen triangle-shaped strands, all set with diamonds and small pearls terminating with tiny light-blue glass beads.

Reverse
The reverse is decorated with exquisite enamel in the champlevé technique showing a mirror image of the front, along with five-petalled, red flowers and green leaves on a light-blue-enamelled ground.

The central decoration is a 'sun and moon' symbol, which correlates with the Rajput belief that they are the descendants of the sun and the moon (the 'Solar race' and the 'Lunar race').

This type of guluband or adyia was a favourite piece of jewellery for Mughal princesses as well as for royal and noble ladies of the court, especially in Rajasthan and Gujarat, and was worn high around the neck. It was the most elaborate ornament of a Rajput bride and would be the centrepiece of her wedding trousseau, symbolising her transition from girl to woman.

Thomas Holbein Hendley mentions this traditional design in Jeypore Enamels: 'The Adiya, a neck or forehead ornament, is of a regal design, reminding one of the Assyrian jewellery. It is peculiar to Marwar, a country in which many relics of ancient art and custom still exist'.

Gold *jungi,* pendant
North India
Eighteenth century

diameter: 5.5 cm

Elaborate gold openworked pendant, *kundan*-set with flat- and rose-cut diamonds. In the centre sits a large emerald, carved in the typical Mughal style, showing an open lotus flower. The pendant is flanked on either side by a peacock with the tail and body set with carved emeralds and cabochon rubies. In the lower part, on either side, is a smaller bird set with a cabochon ruby and carved emeralds. A large irregular emerald bead is attached to the pendant.

The reverse shows high-quality *chitai* work (chased and engraved) which depicts the mirror image of the front.

Gold necklace with seven pendants
Necklace: Gujarat
Nineteenth century
Pendants: Andhra Pradesh
Nineteenth century

Four-row necklace (*makoda*) with seven hollow arrow-shaped pendants. Each pendant is set with a large faceted diamond in a silver mount, surrounded by cabochon rubies and emeralds. A bunch of five small pearls is suspended from each pendant. The reverse of each pendant shows embossed *chitai* work of blooming flowers.

The arrowhead has had great symbolic meaning since ancient times in Indian culture. Even the mere form of the arrowhead was believed to possess the power to protect against evil spirits. To obtain this protection, a pendant in the form of an arrowhead was worn around the neck. Over time, the simple form evolved into a more stylised one, although the extra decoration only reinforces the amulet's auspicious power.

Gold *matha patti*, headdress
Rajasthan
Nineteenth century

weight: 266 g
length, total: 23.5 cm
length, *tikka* with chain: 8.5 cm
width of strap: 3 cm

Traditional gold *karanphul jhumka* (ear pendants) are attached
to a *matha patti*. The two vertical straps are made up of five
horizontal gold bars, all set with diamonds and connected by five
lines of flexible gold chains. Small gold droplets edge both straps.

On top of the two strands is a diamond-set crescent around a
five-petalled diamond-set flower with a cabochon ruby in the
centre. The two crescents have the same fringes of little droplets
as the two strands. The two parts are linked by three gold chains
with a small crescent in the centre, set with rubies and emeralds.
A *tikka* (forehead ornament) of the same design as the two top
finials, is attached to the little crescent.

Further information:
Hendley, *Indian jewellery*, plate 85, illustration 577

Nineteenth-century lithograph of *jahla*, pearl head ornament
S.S. Jacob & T.H. Hendley 1886
Jeypore Enamels, plate 23b

Pacelli, pair of bangles
Rajasthan, Bikaner
Early twentieth century

Flat-formed gold bangles with multicoloured enamel and decorated on the outer edges with thirty-four large flower buds on a stem (*pacelli*), *kundan*-set with diamonds and cabochon rubies.

The enamel work and choice of colours illustrate the typical Bengali workmanship in Rajasthan.

A single row of flower buds on a stem is typical for Rajasthan. A double row of flower buds on a stem is more often seen in Uttar Pradesh.

Further information:
India. Jewels that Enchanted the World, p.72
Untracht, *Traditional Jewelry of India,* p.187, images 353, 354
A Kaleidoscope of Colours, p.92, illustration 68

Hasli
Rajasthan, Bikaner
Nineteenth century

Front
This type of necklace derives its name from the Hindi word *hansuli* (meaning 'collar-bone'). It rests on the collar-bone of the wearer.

The obverse is decorated with a raised gold floral and foliage design, *kundan*-set with foiled diamonds of various weights on a *nil zamin* (dark-blue enamel) ground. The outer perimeter is strung with irregular seed pearls.

The *hasli* has two *makara*-head finials with open mouths in the front, holding a stylised flower set with foiled diamonds and a suspended pearl. The lower side of the mouth is decorated with *sabz zamin* (green enamel), the *makara* heads are decorated with two collars each, which show traces of white and red enamel.

The slightly curved back finials of this *hasli* have, on either side, an oval drop-shaped bead with *kundan*-set diamonds on a *nil zamin* (dark-blue enamel) ground.

Reverse
The reverse side is polychrome enamelled.

A hasli with two makara-head terminals is rare. Makara, a mythical aquatic animal, is usually shown with its mouth wide open and revealing pointed teeth, and with a floral form, ball or pearl emerging from its mouth. The figure plays an important role in Indian mythology and art and the use of mythical and aquatic creatures in jewellery has its origins in the early monuments of the subcontinent, especially in the south.

Further information:
Untracht, *Traditional Jewelry of India*, p.227, illustration 471

Diamond *choti*
Lahore
Late eighteenth/early nineteenth century

length: 8.5 cm
weight: 88 g

Gold *choti* or *chunti* consisting of one large and three smaller
dome-shaped ornaments, *kundan*-set with flat-cut diamonds
and cabochon rubies, decorated with strings of pearls, with tiny
gold bead finials.

A choti *is a hair ornament that is suspended from the end of a woman's
braid.*

Further information:
A Kaleidoscope of Colours, p.52, exhibit number 01
Untracht, *Traditional Jewelry of India*, p.217, illustration 425

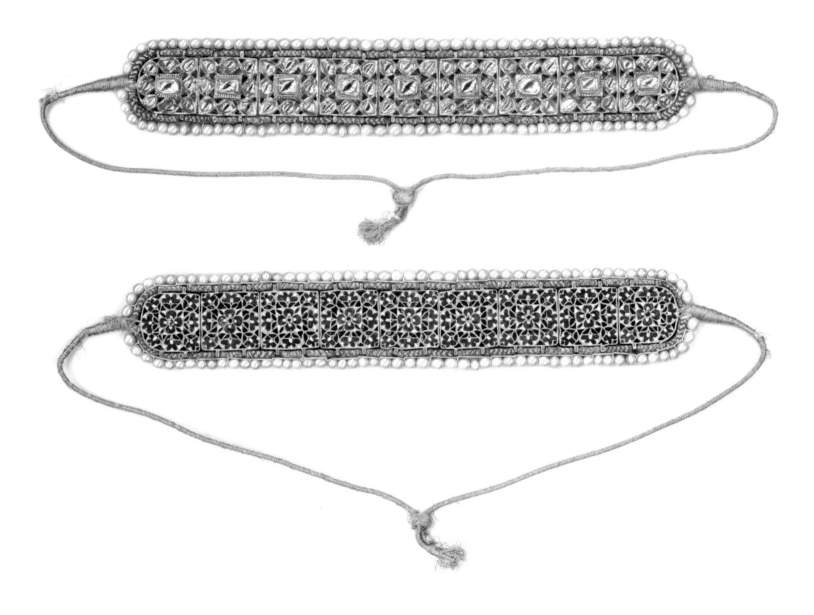

Gold *bazuband,* armlet
Andhra Pradesh, Hyderabad
Nineteenth century

Front
Armlet consisting of seven square gold sections with two
semicircular gold sections as finials, set with eight flat-cut
diamonds surrounding a larger flat-cut diamond in the centre,
all set in the *kundan* technique. The outer edges of each plaque
have, on either side, two small loops through which gold wire
knots link the sections and the 105 pearls that border the
bazuband.

At both ends the cords are gathered together by a coil of
gold-wrapped thread and are connected by a sliding ball.

Reverse
Each section is adorned on the reverse with a floral
arrangement in red, white and green *safed* chalwan enamel.

Pair of *bazubands*
Uttar Pradesh
Late eighteenth century

Delicate gold *bazubands* set with diamonds
and emeralds on foil in *kundan* technique,
complemented with a floral pattern of champlevé
enamel work at the reverse. The *bazubands* are
shown with their original threading.

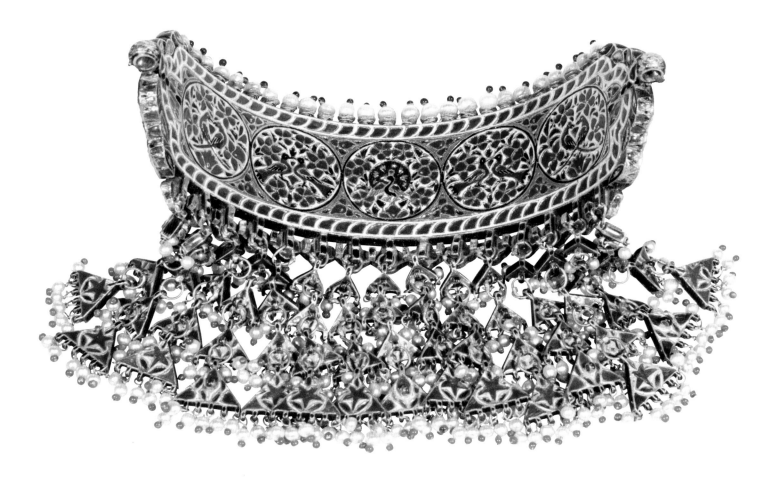

Gold *guluband, arya* or *adiya*, neck ornament
Rajasthan, Bikaner
Nineteenth century

weight: 390 g
height, total: 10.5 cm
height, rigid part only: 3.5 cm
width of rigid part: 18 cm

Front
The rigid part of this *guluband*—gold on a *surma* (wax and lead mix) core is decorated with an exquisite raised gold floral and leaf pattern. The design shows three large rosettes, alternated with smaller rosettes bearing a leaf pattern on top. The whole is *kundan*-set with irregular rose-cut diamonds on a *nil zamin* (blue-enamelled) ground.

The upper edge is decorated with twenty-five small gold cups to which pearls, with dark-blue glass bead finials, are wired. Fifteen diamonds in lozenge settings are attached to the lower edge of the rigid upper part. From these, fifteen strands are suspended, each consisting of four triangles of increasing size, all set with diamonds. Pearls tipped with turquoise-enamelled beads are wired to the lower edge of each triangle.

Reverse
The elaborate champlevé *meenakari* (enamel work) in red, green, dark and light blue on a white ground, shows a pattern of five dark-blue-enamelled circles. A peacock with spread tail surrounded by flowers and leaves, sits in the centre circle, while on either side are two circles, each with birds and a floral and foliage theme. The enamel design is bordered above and below with a white-enamelled band decorated with red-enamelled 'leaves' and light-blue enamel at each inner end of the *guluband*. The reverse of each triangular pendant is decorated with a five-petalled flower and green leaves on a white ground. The edges of the triangles show green enamel.

The use of two different enamel decorations puts this guluband in a certain perspective; the dark-blue-enamelled front set with precious gems and the choice of the enamel decoration at the reverse, showcase the Jaipuri School.

Further information:
Sharma and Varadarajan *Handcrafted Indian Enamel Jewellery*, pp.28, 29

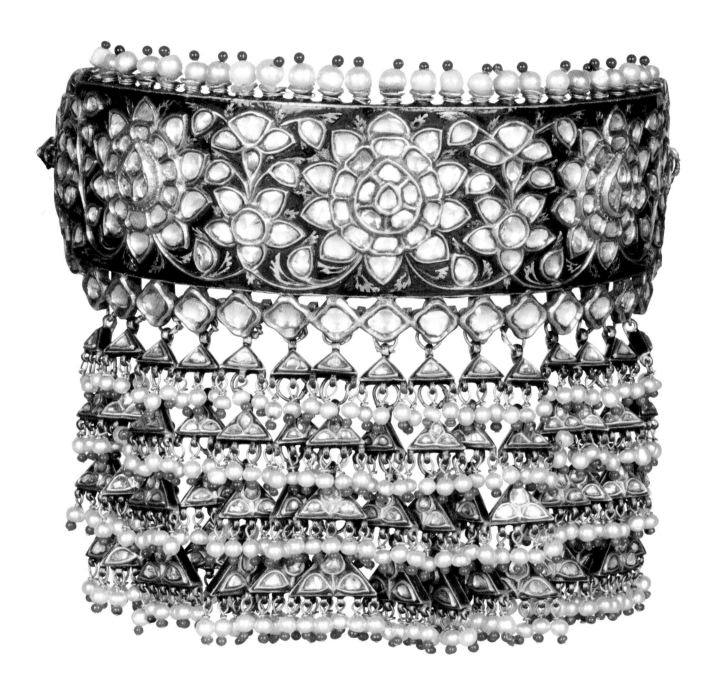

Pair of gold *ganadari, bazubands*
Uttar Pradesh, Benares
Nineteenth century

Pair of *bazubands kundan*-set with foiled diamonds, constructed
as three hinged *tawiz* (amulet) sections, terminating in floral-
design hinges and a cord wrapped with gold thread. The three
tawiz are decorated with *sabz zamin* (green enamel). On the
side and at the reverse are *safed chalwan* enamel of a floral
design in red and green on an opaque white ground.

Bazubands are worn above the elbow.

Gold *jigha*, turban ornament
South India, Tamil Nadu
Early twentieth century

weight: 55 g
heigth: 9 cm
width: 4.3 cm

Gold turban ornament (*jigha*), consisting of two sections, set with precious stones in the *kundan* technique. The upper openwork part shows an elephant head with a curled trunk set with table-cut diamonds, cabochon rubies and a faceted blue sapphire serving as the elephant's eye. The lower openwork part depicts an elephant with a curled trunk set with table-cut diamonds, cabochon rubies, a faceted blue sapphire and an emerald. The *jigha* has a garland of cabochon rubies set in gold collets.

The reverse is of gold sheet with an engraving in Tamil and holds a *tana* for a plume or feathers.

Initially turban ornaments were a symbol of status, rank and power, it was the prerogative of the emperor and his direct entourage (this included his horse). The jigha shown here is an interesting example because of its unusual form. The elephant's voluminous grey body is associated with rain-bearing clouds in the cycle of the life-giving waters, and is therefore seen as a fertility symbol. More importantly, the shape of the elephant head describes the symbol for 'om', which is considered the most sacred word in Hindu literature and is looked upon as the audio-visual representation of the divine, for it is the sound from which the world was created. The mystical syllable 'om', is the symbol of the great God who encompasses the whole universe and goes beyond the periphery of time itself. The majestic elephant is the embodiment of many noble qualities and naturally became the symbol of royalty and power.

Further information:
Untracht, *Traditional Jewelry of India*, first photo in the book
Babur's Heritage, p.88

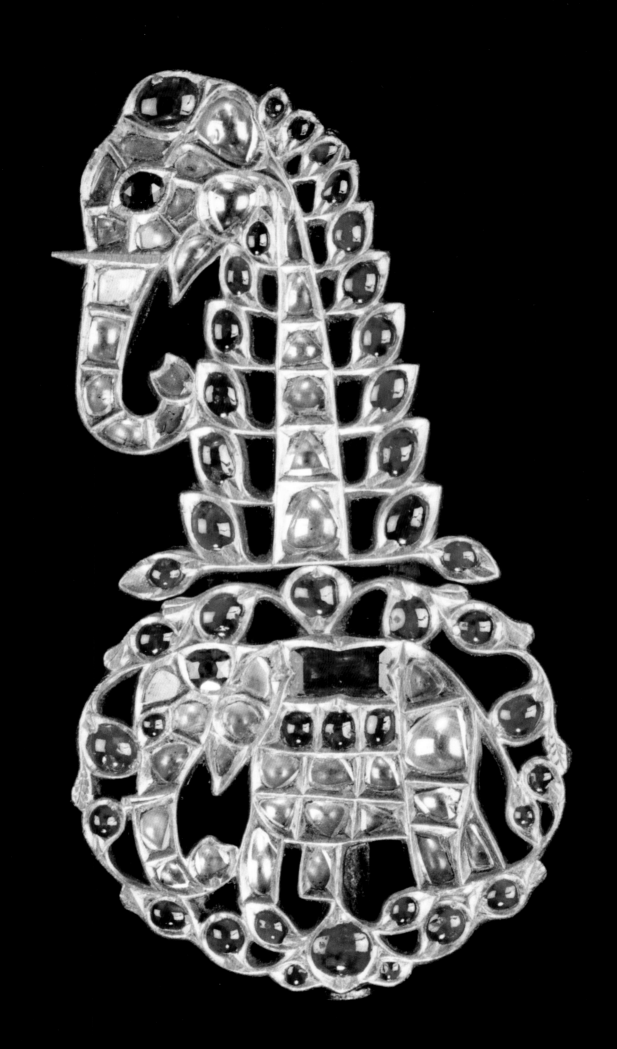

Gold and diamond-set *matha patti*, headdress
Rajasthan, Bikaner
Late eighteenth century

length: 29 cm
width of strap: 3.2 cm
weight: 342 g

An elaborate gold *matha patti* headdress, where the two strands are set with diamonds. The small triangular finials below, are decorated on either side with a stylised bird set with rubies, emeralds and diamonds. On top of each strand is a round plaque depicting a crescent with the sun in the centre, set with diamonds, rubies and emeralds. Each strand is made up of four horizontal gold bars set with diamonds, connected by two rows of pearls and tiny green beads. The edges of both strands are fringed with irregular pearls and tiny, green beads. Suspended beneath are two *karan phool* (ear ornaments—*karan* meaning 'ear'), that consist of two main parts: a roundel, like a flower (*phool*) at the earlobe, from which hangs a small crescent-shaped pendant; from the lower part hang two large, fish-shaped ornaments holding a flower. Suspended below are small drop-shaped pendants with fringes of tiny pearls and green beads.

The reverse of the *matha patti* shows exquisite enamel work in red, white and green with a five-petal flower and bird design on the upper part and three bird motifs on the horizontal bars. The same fish and flower motif from the front of the ear pendants, is repeated on the back in delicate enamel work. The five-petal flower in combination with birds is a typical motif we come across in traditional enamel work from Bikaner.

In India, the wearing of ornate jewellery has always been associated with royalty, particularly during the Mughal dynasty, when the wearing of such opulent jewellery was mainly seen on members of the royal courts and members of Muslim and Hindu noble families. Large karnphul (flower-shaped ear caps) in combination with jumkhi (bell- and dome-shaped pendants), were in high demand. For support, a decorative chain could be added; together, the whole piece was called a matha patti.

Bikaner has a great tradition of splendid court life and its history dates back to 1486 when a Rathore prince, Rao Bikaji, founded this desert kingdom. The strategic location of Bikaner on the ancient caravan routes that came from West/Central Asia, made it a prime trade centre and the kingdom flourished. The magnificent palaces and forts, created with great delicacy in reddish-pink sandstone, bear testimony to its rich historical and architectural legacy.

Further information:
Babur's Heritage, pp.87, 88
Bhandari, *Costume, Textiles and Jewellery of India*, pp.85, 104

Gold *gajredar,* bracelets
Rajasthan
Late nineteenth century

Each *gajredar* consists of five large hollow half-dome-shaped elements with tiny beads individually soldered to the surface. A bar with an anti-clockwise screw in the centre, supports the exquisite terminals in the form of two parrots, each set with diamonds and two rubies.

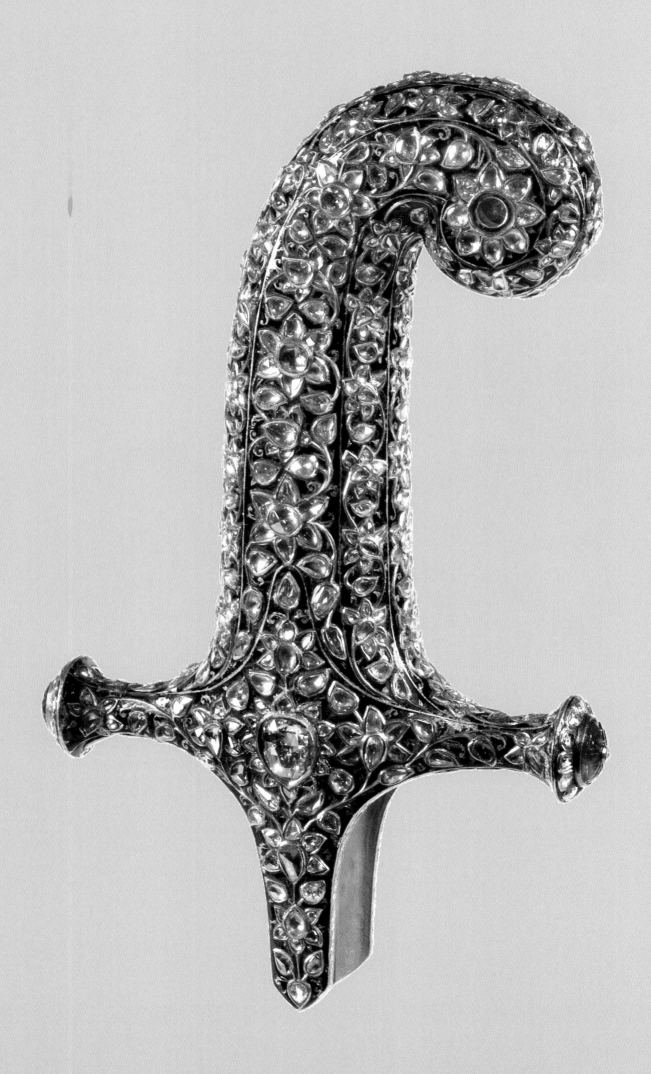

Gold hilt
North India
Nineteenth century

height: 19 cm
weight: 455 g

Gold hilt on a *surma* (combination of wax and lead) core with
a curved pommel, decorated with a raised gold floral and leaf
design and set with foiled rose-cut Golconda diamonds of various
weights in the *kundan* style. The hilt shows a three-dimensional *nil
zamin* (dark-blue enamel) *sab jagah ko mina* (enamel all around).

The finials are set with a cabochon ruby carved into a lotus motif.

A small diamond is affixed to one ruby. The outer line on the
lower part shows traces of light-blue enamel.

The splendour and abundance at the Mughal courts grew constantly,
particularly through the regal custom of giving and receiving presents
when officials presented themselves at court.

It was equally the custom for the emperor to offer lavishly decorated and
bejewelled presents, even elephants and horses, to his loyal followers, in
order to secure their loyalty.

*All this opulence attracted foreign craftsmen to the royal karkhanas (workshops),
resulting in a hybrid of Indian, Persian and Western style and techniques.*

*Indian arms and armoury often show this blend of foreign influences
combined with the traditional style, since jewelled daggers and swords were
a symbol of status and rank, hilts took on an additional importance. They
were made of ivory, jade, nephrite, rock crystal, silver, iron or gold and were
decorated with gold, enamel and set with precious gems.*

This superbly worked hilt is unmistakably from a royal workshop.

Further information:
Babur's Heritage, p.73

Turban ornament
North India, West Bengal, late nineteenth century

height: 6.1 cm

Elaborate gold and silver turban ornament, composed of an openworked gold cast, slightly curved and in a pear-shaped form. A large pear-shaped rose-cut diamond *kundan*-set in a raised collet, is bordered by a thin line of tiny cabochon pyrope garnets. The central diamond is surrounded by seven smaller leaf-shaped rose-cut diamonds and one horizontal oval-shaped diamond below, all *kundan*-set in the same raised collets. On either side of the jewel and below the oval-shaped diamond are four tiny cabochon pyrope garnets.

The gold jewel is bordered with a silver raised lower section, set with thirteen pear-shaped rose-cut diamonds. The silver front part is covered by a gold plate at the reverse. Gold suspension loops on either side are for cords or chains to run through to tighten the turban. The reverse is undecorated.

Further information:
Van Gelder, *The Origin of Quality*

Blue Sapphire
Sauri Ratna, *Gem of Shani*

*Because of its association with the turbulent and powerful Shani,
Hindus wear jewellery set with blue sapphires with great caution
and only after having consulted their astrologer*

Sanipriya is Sanskrit for 'blue sapphire' and is associated with the planet Saturn. In
Vedic astrology it is said that anyone who worships *Shani* (Saturn) and wears a *neelam*
(blue sapphire) will receive his blessings; the blue sapphire is traditionally associated
with love and purity. Because of its association with the turbulent and powerful *Shani*,
Hindus wear jewellery set with blue sapphires with great caution and only after having
consulted their astrologer. The exception for the use of blue sapphires is that it may
be worn in combination with other precious stones as seen in the *nava ratna* (nine
stones) or *nauratan* arrangement. The presence of blue sapphires is more usually
found in objects and works of art commissioned or owned by Muslims than by
Hindus. Sapphires were also among the gems that adorned the Peacock Throne. The
deep blue variety of corundum is also called *sauri ratna* and has been regarded as one
of the *maharatnani* (five great gems) of Indian astrology since ancient times.

Gold *pankhi*, fan-shaped pendant
Andhra Pradesh

width: 4 × 3.2 cm
weight: 21 g

Gold *pankhi* (fan-shaped pendant) depicting blue sapphire *vishnupada* or *pagalia* in the centre,
surrounded by nine *polki*, rose-cut diamonds set in the *kundan* technique. The pendant has
two suspension loops on top and a smaller loop below and shows a carved gold garland at
the front and at the reverse.

Pairs of feet such as these are called pagalia. *The feet on this pendant must have been inspired by the
Vishnupada symbol and commissioned by Krishna devotees. Krishna is the eighth incarnation of Lord Vishnu.
Jains also worship feet but they never appear as an ornament. Gaya, a city in Bihar, has a famous Hindu
temple, built in 1787 and dedicated to Lord Vishnu, called Vishnu Mandir, marked by 40-centimetre-long
footprints (Vishnupada) imprinted in solid rock and surrounded by a silver-plated basin.*

Further information:
Van Gelder, *The Origin of Quality*, p.9

The name sapphire comes from the Greek word *sapphirus*, meaning 'blue'. Early Sanskrit texts mention Sri Lanka as an important source and divide blue sapphire into two varieties: *indranila*, which is a precious deep blue colour; and *mahanila,* which is a darker blue.

Sapphire is one of the three gem varieties of corundum; it is identical to ruby in every attribute except for its colour and it has fewer inclusions than ruby. Its colours range almost the entire spectrum, from colourless to green, black, violet, yellow and the rare pinkish-orange colour which is called *padmaraga* (also commonly known as *padparadscha*) in Sinahalese. The name *padmaraga* is derived from Sanskrit and means 'lotus colour' (*padma* 'lotus' and *raga* 'colour'). It is believed that the orange-coloured sapphire is a solar stone and connected with Mars, bringing warmth and physical comfort. It is the quantities of oxides of iron, chromium and titanium with a slight mixture of cobalt that result in the blue colour and like many corundums, sapphire has a good lustre. Its hardness is 9 on the Mohs scale, second only to diamond.

Sri Lanka is the most ancient source of sapphires in the world. The centre of sapphire mining was in the south-east part of the island near the city of Ratnapura; its name is derived from Sanskrit, *ratna* meaning 'gems' and *pura* meaning 'city'. At the time, Sri Lanka already had experienced gemstone cutters and they preferred to export their gemstones cut and polished, instead of as rough stones.

Since the sixteenth century blue sapphire has also been mined in Mogok, Burma (Myanmar) and intensively traded with India. These two countries became the most important suppliers of blue sapphires during Mughal times, until the late nineteenth century when, in 1881, blue sapphires were discovered in Kashmir by accident, as the result of a landslide.

Traditional Hindu society is divided into four ranks, or *varnas* (not to be confused with the much more highly differentiated caste system). These ranks correspond to the traditional culture of grouping sapphires in terms of their qualities:

Brahmin	brilliant blue colour
Kshatriya	slightly reddish tinge in a blue sapphire
Vaishya	deep blue colour in a slightly white stone
Shudra	blue colour with some dark tinge in the stone

Kashmir Sapphire

Sapphires were first discovered in a remote region in the Great Himalayan mountains of north-western India in 1881, or early 1882. Located in the small Kudi Valley in the Padar region of Kashmir, it is said that the area was discovered by accident; a landslip had laid bare the rocks beneath the soil and had disclosed the presence of the gems. Historians have provided us with several versions of the discovery of the corundum deposits, among them Valentine Ball (1885). He dated the findings to ca. 1879 or 1880, but T. D. La Touche (1890) gives another time-line: 1881 or 1882.

La Touche (Deputy Superintendent, Geological Survey of India) was a trained geologist despatched to the site in September of that year, who wrote the first scientific description of that area. He mentioned two different sites: the 'old mine' and one found later, the 'new mine'. All the large, fine sapphires were taken from the 'old mine' in the period 1881–1887, rendering the subsequent results of the 'new mine' rather disappointing. A. Graham Young (1882) provided what is probably the only detailed description of the 'old mine' material.

At first no-one had any idea of the value of the stones. It was a local from the Lahol area who picked up a small sapphire and sold it to a trader, who took it to Simla, where its value was recognised. At some point it attracted the attention of Maharadja Ranbir Singh (1857–1885), ruler of the Princely State of Jammu and Kashmir, and soon news spread of the gems, their quality and value. The methods of mining in the Kashmir region were primitive, due to the remote location, harsh weather and altitude (approximately 4,500 m) which restricted mining to the summer months. The characteristic feature of Kashmir sapphires is their velvety cornflower blue, or the bright navy satiny colour, absolutely clear and pure, and perfectly transparent. The reputation of top-quality sapphires from Kashmir is second to none. The gem is sometimes called *Mayur Neelam,* as the colour resembles the colour of the neck of the male peacock. Kashmir sapphires are rare and have a high monetary value. It is said that their quality sets the standard by which all blue sapphires are evaluated. Kashmir sapphires are extremely rare to find today and when found they are set in antique and old pieces of jewellery. Unfortunately, due to political instability and disputes in the region, mining no longer happens and the area is considered to be entirely depleted.

Famous Sapphires

Three of the world's largest faceted blue sapphires, including the 466-carat Blue Giant of the Orient, came from the mines of Sri Lanka.

The Blue Giant of the Orient
© Denis Hayoun, Art Photo / Diode SA

The Blue Giant of the Orient

Mined in the Ratnapura district of Sri Lanka in 1907, the rough stone weighed approximately 600 carats, as reported by the Sri Lankan newspaper *Morning Leader*. After cutting, the finished cushion-cut gem weighed 466 carats. The stone was then sold to an anonymous American collector and was not heard of until 2004, when it was again sold to an anonymous buyer through a sale by auction.

Logan Blue

A 422.99-carat sapphire of a natural colour, mined in Sri Lanka; the cushion-cut gem was donated in 1960 by Mrs John A. Logan to the Smithsonian Institute. The Logan Blue is the heaviest mounted gem in the National Gem Collection. It has a beautiful medium-soft violet-blue colour and exceptional clarity. The stone is on display in the Gem Gallery at the National Museum of Natural History in Washington, DC.

The Logan Blue
©2017 National Museum of Natural History, National Gem Collection, Smithsonian

Padparadscha Sapphire

A uniquely hued sapphire from Sri Lanka, weighing 100 carats and with a pinkish orange-salmon colour. It is possibly the finest large fancy sapphire in the world, and is on display at the American Museum of Natural History in New York.

Star Sapphires

The presence of a star is a rare phenomenon in the world of coloured gemstones and is highly favoured by the people of the orient. The mineral rutile gives the gem its star effect. Tiny fibres of rutile in a three-fold pattern reflect the incoming light in a star pattern; this effect is called asterism. For centuries Sri Lanka has been the greatest source of quality blue star sapphires. Whilst Burma (Myanmar) does not produce as many blue star sapphires, it is said to be the source of stones of the best colour. Kashmir does not produce star sapphires. Star sapphires are mostly cut and polished as cabochons in order to enhance the display of the asterism. Occasionally, stars with up to twelve rays are found, usually occurring when two different sets of inclusions are found within the same stone. The value of a star sapphire depends on several criteria; the weight of the stone, the colour, visibility and the intensity of the asterism.

Famous Star Sapphires

Star of Asia

The Star of Asia, once in the possession of the Maharaja of Jodhpur, is a large 330-carat cabochon-cut star sapphire currently located at the Smithsonian National Museum of Natural History.

The gem is noted for its significant size and is considered to be one of the largest of its type. It is also noted for its rich colour and clear star. The stone originates from the Mogok mines of Burma.

The Star of Bombay

Another great example of a dome-shaped blue star sapphire (182 carats). This fabulous stone originated in Sri Lanka where it was cut and polished by traditional gem-cutters. The gem is on display at the National Museum of Natural History in Washington DC.

Star of Asia
©2017 National Museum of Natural History,
National Gem Collection, Smithsonian

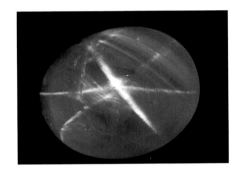

The Star of Bombay
©2017 National Museum of Natural History,
National Gem Collection, Smithsonian

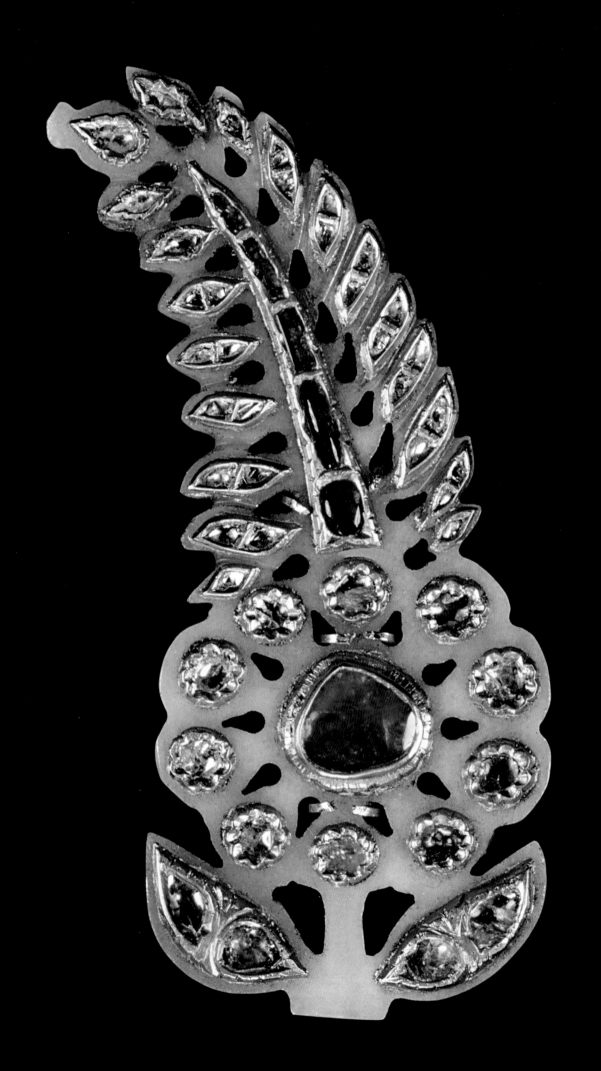

Emerald

Marakatam, *Gem of Budha*

Tears of the moon

Within the context of Indian astrology, emerald is referred to as *panna*. It is the gem connoting the planet Mercury as well as being one of the gems in the *nava ratna* arrangement. Emerald is the green variety of beryl, a beryllium aluminium silicate. In nature it commonly occurs in the crystal habit that is known as a hexagonal prism. Beryl in its purest form is colourless and has a value of 7.5–8 on the Mohs scale of mineral hardness. Traces of chromium and vanadium create the purest green, as seen in emeralds from Colombia, South America. Emerald is relatively brittle, so great care is needed during cutting, setting and in preserving the stone.

In Sanskrit, emerald is known as *markat* or *marakata*: *mara* meaning 'desert', *kata* meaning 'seacoast', a specific area situated between the Nile and the Red Sea in southern Egypt. From its Persian name *zamurrad* came its Greek name *smaragdos*, which became *smaralda* when translated into Latin, and finally took shape as 'emerald' in the early sixteenth century.

Although common beryl is abundant in India, emerald does not appear to have been found there, although it was mentioned in the Agastimata (a Sanskrit poetic

Jigha, turban ornament
North India
Nineteenth century

height: 9 cm
width: 4 cm

A monochromatic white nephrite *jigha*, turban ornament.

In the centre is an irregular triangular form, set with a green-foiled emerald in *kundan*, surrounded by ten floret-style foiled *kundan*-set diamonds. Below the centre on either side are two leaf-shaped decorations, each set with two foiled table-cut diamonds. The upper part of the *jigha* is set with foiled flat diamonds and foiled emeralds.

The back of the *jigha* is carved in a floral design, and behind the central triangle is a socket for a plume of feathers (the lower tapering part is missing).

Further information
Hendley, *Indian Jewellery*, plate 4, illustration 15
Jaffer, *Beyond Extravagance*, pp.74, 104, illustration 34
Crespo, *Jóias da Carreirada India*, p.51, figure 22

composition of 322 verses from the eighth century) as one of the five *Maharatnani* (the five greater gems) which also names 'eight varieties of emeralds, the finest of them being transparent, without dust, pure as a drop of dew on a lotus leaf.'[1] No ancient jewellery set with emeralds has been found, but there are many references to it in the Mahabharata (Sanskrit literature from the first to the third centuries AD).

Until the Spanish captured the Colombian mines, the only sources of emeralds in the Ancient World were the Sikait-Zabara mines in Egypt, Habachtal (Austria) and the Swat Valley along the border between Pakistan and Afghanistan. This was verified by research carried out by Gaston Giuliani in 2000 when he analysed the oxygen-isotope content of emerald jewellery from a Gallic-Roman burial mound: 'oxygen is a principal element of emerald, the proportion of stable oxygen-isotopes will be unique to a particular locality.' A combination of further techniques, Giuliani's work and that of a team of French researchers, has enabled the world's major emerald mines to be categorised according to their oxygen-isotope analysis results, making it possible to determine with certainty the origin of any emerald.[2]

Emeralds from any given district, or mine, will have distinct 'fingerprints' determined by the oxygen-isotope content. French geochemists evaluated many emeralds from known localities, then compared the results with emeralds whose origins were not known. Their analysis of a selection of emerald-set artifacts from the Gallo-Roman period to the eighteenth century indicated that, historically, artisans worked with emeralds that originated from deposits supposedly discovered in the twentieth century.[3]

In antiquity, Swat Valley emeralds, and those from Egypt, were traded via the Silk Route. Together with emeralds from Austria, they were the only source of gem-quality emeralds, until the discovery of South America.

The Egyptian mines supplied Byzantium, Babylon and Rome. The region was known as the Mons Smaragdus, or Emerald Mountains. The grouping of mines became known generically as the Wadi Gimal or Cleopatra Mines, situated twenty kilometres north of Aswan and probably worked some 2000 years BC. The Egyptian emeralds were fairly small, light in colour, often cloudy and rather inferior in quality, but still Egypt had a monopoly on export trade to the East and the Mediterranean. Their export monopoly was broken in the early sixteenth century as a result of the Spanish conquest of Central and South America.

Emeralds from Colombia

One of the first mines to be discovered in 1538 by the Spaniard Don Gonzalo Jiménez de Quesada was Somondoco (meaning 'god of the green stones'), now Chivor, north-east of Santa Fe de Bogotá. Don Gonzalo was presented with nine 'green stones' by the inhabitants of the town of Guachetá. Later, ca. 1558, some 125 kilometres from Chivor, they learned about another very fruitful mine, located in the region inhabited by the Muzo tribe. The Muzo were warriors by nature, and cannibals, and they fiercely resisted conquest. It took the Spaniards from 1538 to 1558 to establish a small fortified settlement in the area. In the same area, approximately ten kilometres away, they also discovered the Cosquez mines. It is said that the world's most beautiful emeralds came, and still do come, from the mine at Muzo. Some of the stones from the Muzo district had a warm velvety bluish-green appearance which was highly prized.

The Spanish fleets brought back fabulous emeralds from their South American colonies, but gold was much more important to them than the magnificent green stones. It wasn't long before the Portuguese started to bargain for the emeralds, because they were aware of the riches of India and were especially eager to trade the emeralds for their diamonds. Emeralds from the New World entered the old trade routes, both maritime and land-based, not only from Spain but also from the Spanish colonies in the Philippines. The trade soon dominated Europe, the Middle East and reached the Portuguese trade enclaves of Goa and Diu on the Indian west coast.

The Portuguese, aware of the Mughals' devotion to high-quality jewellery and precious stones, introduced the emeralds at court and to the provincial nobility. The superior quality and immense size of the emeralds from the Colombian mines gave the Mughals the utmost delight. Because of their 'milky' transparency they were called 'tears of the moon'. It is said that the first emeralds from Colombia to reach the subcontinent were presented to Emperor Akbar the Great (1556–1605) whereupon it took him and his nine royal counsellors many days to assess the quality, weights and sizes. According to Hindu custom, the royal astrologer was also present to determine the auspicious meaning of the gems.

In 1607, William Hawkins commanded the ship *Hector* for the East India Company on a voyage to Surat and Aden. Emperor Jehangir had allowed him to reside in the palace at Agra from 1609 to 1611, where he witnessed the weighing of unmounted emeralds among other loose precious stones: 'Emperor Jehangir had one and a half batmans of loose diamonds (over 180,000 carats) none smaller than two carats. He had five batmans of unmounted emeralds. This illustrates the vast amount of emerald riches flowing from South America to India just 50 years after the Spanish gained control of the Muzo mine.'[4]

Most of the Mughal Emperors were gemstone connoisseurs, especially Emperor Shah Jahan (1628–1658) who willingly spent enormous sums of gold to acquire these fantastic green marvels from the then so-called 'New World'. India became by far the main market for the largest and finest of the fabulous emeralds of Colombia, and since then emeralds have been associated with royalty and status. Many of the Mughal military expeditions were financed by the sale of large emeralds. The belief that a good-quality emerald would change colour when it came into contact with poison, encouraged the Mughal rulers' use of emerald drinking cups; jade and celadon were reputed to have the same powers.

The colour green is considered to be the traditional colour of Islam; it symbolises life and nature. In Islamic culture, the colours green and gold are the colours of paradise. Emerald beads made into Muslim rosaries (strings of prayer beads: *tasbih* in Arabic, *subhah* in Persian) were also sent to the holy places Mecca and Medina as votive offerings. The Mughals, being Muslim, valued emeralds second to diamonds. Still, it is no coincidence that the Imperial Treasury contained more loose emeralds than it did diamonds and rubies together.

Emerald Sources in India

Emerald has been known in India since prehistoric times, but the modern practice of emerald mining developed only after 1943–44 when the Geological Survey of India first identified the green crystals as emeralds near the small village of Kaliguman in southern Rajasthan.

Areas producing a certain commercial quality of gemstone today are in the region of Ajmer near Rajgarh village and Gamguda and Tekhi areas of Udaipur. The quality of these emeralds is a little disappointing, as they are dark in colour and display rather shimmering inclusions.

The mineral was mined manually by the opencast method; the pits were worked at shallow depths and the stones collected during mining were sorted according to quality, shape and size and deposited with the State Government under the supervision of DMG (Department of Mines & Geology) officials and mine owners. In the light of Gaston Guiliani's research, some have wondered if the Rajasthan emerald mine of India, 'officially' discovered in the 1950s, might have produced some of the old emeralds used in Indian jewellery. So far, however, none has been identified in any jewellery from ancient sites.[5] Jaipur in Rajasthan continues to be the main location for skillful cutting and polishing of emeralds into faceted or rounded form for use in jewellery. The rough stones are sorted to determine the angles at which facets can be cut. They may be sawn or polished in any direction depending on the shape, colour or size to be retained. After the shape and size are determined, the next process is faceting and polishing to achieve maximum internal reflection, enhancing the beauty of the stone. In the nineteenth and twentieth centuries emeralds were generally given a step—or cabochon—cut. Like other gemstones, emerald also depends upon the four C's—**c**ut, **c**arat, **c**larity and **c**olour. The colour of emeralds has always been the standard for grading all green-coloured gems.

It is interesting that in the state of Kerala large emerald beads are seldom worn close to the neck because, they are considered harmful.

Carved and Inscribed Emeralds

Fine, hardstone, relief carving techniques from the early Islamic world were also applied to pieces of gemstone jewellery. During Mughal times, large emeralds were sometimes inscribed in the Persian language, using Arabic letters, with passages from the holy Qur'an, as Arabic was considered the language of culture and prevailed at court. The inscribing and carving was made by chosen lapidaries after consultation with astrologers for suitable dates and times. The inscriptions, made on the surface of the stone in intaglio, were either made so the viewer could read the text in the obverse, or with the text reversed so the text could be read when used as a seal. It was believed that such inscriptions, titles, words and symbols could protect the wearer against demons and diseases; thus the emerald was also worn as a powerful amulet or protective talisman, on the left upper arm close to the heart with the inscribed side against the skin. The other (visible) side would be decorated with an exuberant floral pattern, typical of the naturalistic decoration of the period, reflecting the Mughal love of nature, and also to appeal to the taste of the wearer.

Equestrian Portrait of Safdar Khan
India (Deccan, Hyderabad), ca. 1790–1810

Emerald necklace
Private collection

By the seventeenth century the master carvers in Jaipur (Rajasthan) and Gujarat were producing wonderful carved emeralds with beautiful calligraphy on one side and intricate floral patterns on the other, to bring out the full colour and beauty of the stone. Large emeralds were rare, even unknown, until their discovery in the sixteenth century by the Spanish conquistadores. Royalty and wealthy nobility during the Mughal era, as well as other great Islamic empires such as the Safavid Persians and the Ottoman Turks, rapidly became passionate collectors of these magnificent works of art, which they wore and also gave as gifts. Carved, as well as inscribed, emeralds became some of the most characteristic and sumptuous jewels from the golden age of the Mughal period which reached its climax under Emperor Shah Jahan and his son and successor, Emperor Aurengzeb (1658–1707).

Cut and Forms

The best-quality emeralds are almost universally fashioned in the 'trap' or 'step'-cut style with corners truncated, giving an elongated octagonal outline, a style which has become known as emerald cut. In traditional Indian jewellery we see hexagonal, cabochon, cushion form and pear-shaped. Other shapes come from irregularly formed crystals in the beryl. All emerald contains inclusions, even the finest gem, and although these might not be visible to the naked eye, they will show up under a 10x, 20x or 40x lens.

Hexagonal Cut

During Mughal times the large six-sided (*chakoni*) and sometimes eight-sided (*athkoni*) plaques became popular. These typical emerald-cut forms derived from the shape of the natural hexagonal prism with a pinacoid termination. The naturally symmetrical six-sided form could be altered to an octagon with minimal loss simply by removing two opposite corners of the hexagon.[6] The flat surface of the emerald was ideal for carving in low relief and inscribing.

Beads

A popular form of emeralds in traditional Indian jewellery is tumbled beads, most of them in irregular form, made from smaller emerald crystals which preserves maximum stone bulk. The stones were tumble-polished using a typical Indian technique. Imperial portraits (during the reign of Jahangir, 1605–1627, and Shah Jahan, 1628–1658) often show emperors wearing large pearl necklaces with drilled, polished emerald beads as spacers and large earrings fashioned in the same manner.

Melon Form

Another emerald bead form is known as the melon form (*kharbuja*). Emerald beads of that shape are often carved, and reffered to as *kharbuja kheredar,* a technique that involves carving the surface with parallel grooves ending at the bead's drilled hole.

Tawiz-shaped

Emeralds were also cut in an elliptical shape and worn as a *tawiz* pendant. *Tawiz* means 'talisman' or 'amulet'.

Famous Emeralds

Taj Mahal Emerald

A great example of the hexagonal cut is the beautiful Colombian gemstone named Taj Mahal (weight approximately 141.13 carats). It is one of the most treasured jewels in Indian history. Sublime and very detailed, it is carved in raised relief on one side, with stylised chrysanthemum, lotus and Mughal-style poppy flowers, leaves and buds in the asymmetrical foliage that typifies the naturalistic decoration of the period and reflects the Mughals' love of nature. The reverse of the emerald is undecorated, except for a single wheel-cut line. It is a strong indication of Indian lapidaries' skill during the peak of Mughal rule. Their standards have rarely been surpassed in India.

The name of this precious emerald is derived from its intricately carved surface of blooms and other foliage that mirrors the decoration of the Taj Mahal in Agra. The Taj Mahal Emerald is one of three large Mughal emeralds that featured prominently as centrepieces in Cartier's Collier Berenice (necklace or shoulder ornament) during the Exposition des Arts Decoratif et Industriel Modernes at Paris in 1925. The Taj Mahal Emerald is now part of the Benjamin Zucker Family Collection in New York.

The Mogul Mughal, reversed and obversed
© The Museum of Islamic Art, Doha

The Mogul Mughal

This remarkably large, rectangular-cut and splendidly carved emerald (217.8 carats) is considered to be one of the largest emeralds known (5.1 x 3.8 cm). The Mogul Mughal is unique among emeralds of the Mughal period that bear a date. On one side the emerald is inscribed with a Shi'ite inscription invoking God to bless the twelve imams and the *hijra* date AH 1107 (AD 1695) which places it within the reign of Emperor Aurengzeb (1658–1707), the last of the Great Mughal Rulers. However, the Mughal rulers were Sunni, whereas the inscription is Shi'ite, making it likely that it belonged not to Emperor Aurengzeb, but to one of his courtiers, of whom many were of Shi'a Deccan or Persian origin and were familiar with the Shi'ite formulas at the Deccani courts.

The inscription on the top reads:

'The Merciful One, The Compassionate One'; the inscription on the other side reads:

O God, God bless Muhammad and ´Ali and Fatima and al-Husain and al-Hasan and ´Ali and Muhammad and Ja´far and Musa 1107 [1695'] and ´Ali and Muhammad and 'Ali and al- Husaini and the steadfast Mahdi.[7]

The side with the inscription in intaglio was worn facing inwards, against the skin. The obverse side is adorned with a typical Mughal-style floral pattern with a central rosette flanked by large and small poppy flowers. The emerald has drilled holes for attachments on four sides. This is the only known carved and dated emerald of the glorious Mughal period. The gemstone is part of Qatar's national collection of Mughal Jewellery and is on display at the Museum of Islamic Art in Doha, Qatar.

1. Taank, *Indian Gemmology*, p.29.

2. Ringsrud, *Emeralds*, pp. 229, 230.

3. Guiliani, *et al.*, 'Oxygen Isotopes and Emerald Trade Routes Since Antiquity', pp.631–3.

4. Ringsrud, *Emeralds*, p.49.

5. Ringsrud, *Emeralds*, p.231.

6. Untracht, *Traditional Jewelry of India*, p.330.

7. Welch, *India: Art and Culture, 1300–1900*, p.273.

Gold *gop* chain, necklace
Rajasthan, Udaipur and Bundi district
Necklace, nineteenth century
Centrepiece, early twentieth century

Double *gop* chain, or *kanthi,* consisting of two hollow flexible loop-in-loop gold chains with a centre ornament, set with *parab* flat-cut diamonds, one large cabochon emerald and four cabochon rubies. Four small bands, soldered together, hold the two chains in place.

This type of necklace is worn by men.

Headdress
Tamil Nadu
Late nineteenth century

Gold headdress, in the form of a crescent, set with eighteen foiled cabochon rubies. Attached to the crescent are fifteen leaf-shaped ornaments, interspersed with irregular pearls and set with foiled cabochon rubies, emeralds and faceted diamonds.

This crescent ornament is worn on the back of the head in combination with an ornament above and below and a hair jewel attached to the braid.

Further information:
Krishna, *Arts and Crafts of Tamil Nadu*, p. 72, photo on the left

Forehead ornament
North India
Late nineteenth century

Gold on a *lac* core forehead or turban ornament representing
a double crescent, channel-set with emeralds. The centre shows
elaborate open floral work, *kundan*-set with flat-cut diamonds and
three pearls on top. At the back are three suspension loops, to
which cords or chains may have been attached to fasten the jewel.

This forehead ornament is called a *tikka* or *kashka*, and is worn
on the forehead, suspended by a chain from the central hair
parting. It is also possible that this particular ornament was worn
as a turban jewel.

Further information:
Jaffer, *Beyond Extravagance*, pp.170, 196, illustration 81
Sharma and Varadarajan, *Handcrafted Indian Enamel Jewellery*, p.72

Gold *kanthi,* necklace
Rajasthan, Udaipur, Jaisalmer, Nagur
Nineteenth century

Gop chain, consisting of six double loop-in-loop chains. Four gold
bands decorated with little flowers hold the chains in place. The
necklace is embellished with three large gold units, all set with
cabochon rubies, emeralds and faceted white sapphires.

This kind of short kanthi *was worn by men on their* sherwani, *a long coat-like
garment associated with the aristocracy of the Indian subcontinent.*

*There are four major types of loop-in-loop chain. These are chains in which
stretched circlets of wire are folded and linked together in different series.
When linked together in various ways, a variety of chain types are produced.*

Further information:
Jenkins and Keene, *Islamic Jewelry in the Metropolitan Museum of Art,* p. 144

Gold necklace
Rajasthan, Bikaner
Nineteenth century

Necklace composed of gold oblong-shaped segments, each
kundan-set with white sapphires and suspended emerald drops.

The reverse is entirely enamelled with *sabz zamin* (green enamel).

Gold *juda,* head ornament
South India
Early nineteenth century

weight: 342 g
diameter, top part: 6.5 cm

Elaborate gold dome-shaped head ornament (*juda*) with a
suspended fringe of triangle-shaped pendants in a spreading
network. The whole is *kundan*-set with table-cut diamonds,
cabochon rubies and emeralds on coloured foil with suspended
pearls.

*This type of ladies' head ornament was designed to be worn at the back of
the head.*

Further information:
Babur's Heritage, p.67
Van Cutsem, *A World of Head Ornaments,* p.105

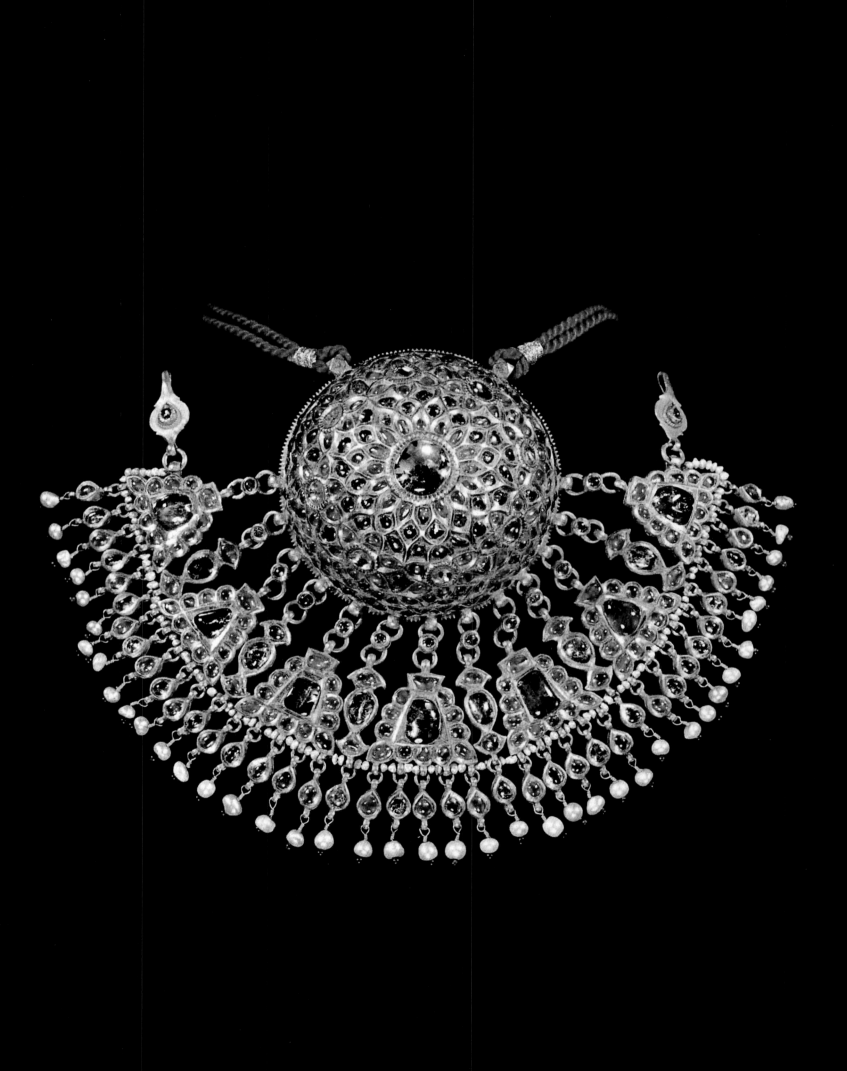

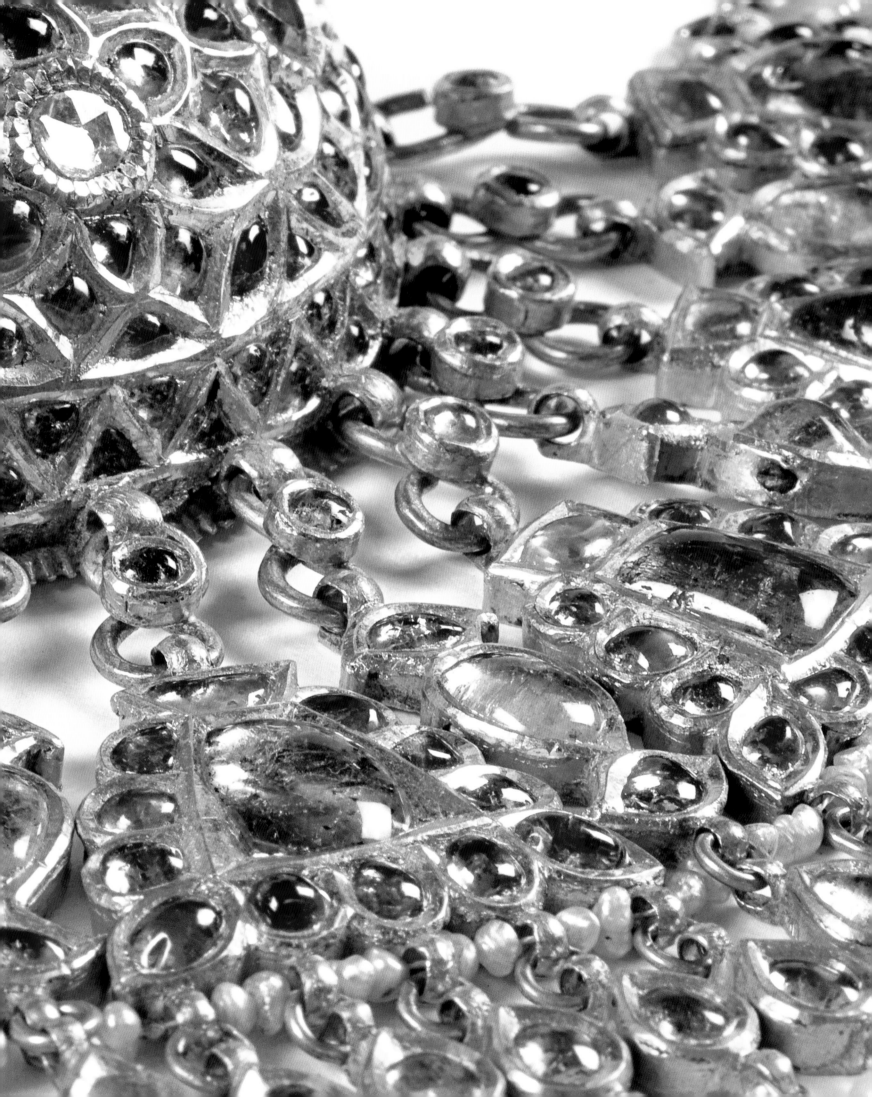

DEVEDASCHIE,

OF INDIASCHE DANSERESSE.

Jacob Gottfried Haafner (1754–1809) mentioned this type of headdress as being worn by *devedaschie* (Dutch) or *devadasis*, temple dancers in Tamil Nadu.

Centuries ago, a practice developed whereby some women were ceremoniously married to a deity by the symbolic tying of a necklace, hence they became wives of God, and were called devadasis. *They lived in and around Hindu temples, performing duties at the temple and participating in religious rites. The relationship between dance, religion and worship of the deities formed the foundation upon which the entire structure of the devadasi system was built. They also performed dances and music for the élite at private family functions, such as marriages, where their presence was considered auspicious. The devadasi system was prevalent all over India. They were taught to read and write and received intensive training from Nattuvanaras, the dance masters. They preserved the classical dances of India, such as the former Sadir dance, (now known as the Bharatnatyam in Tamil Nadu) and the Odissi Dance of Temples in Orissa, where the dancers were known as* maharis.

Further information:
Haafner, *Exotische Liefde*, p.50.
Archer, *Company Paintings*, 34, 7 (2)
Babur's Heritage, p.67
Van Cutsem, *A World of Head Ornaments*, p.109

Spinel

Balas Ruby

*A hill at Chatlan was broken open by an earthquake and within
a white rock in the fracture was found the 'Laal-Bedaschan'*

A love of precious stones was shared by all Mughal emperors; their chronicles
and memoirs contain many references to gemstones such as emeralds, rubies and
diamonds, which they appreciated for their lustre and colour. One stone particularly
favoured by the Mughals was the pinkish-red balas ruby.

Miniature paintings reveal the Mughals' fondness for precious stones and their love
for the colours red and green, especially when combined with pearls. Akbar, Jahangir,
Shah Jahan and Aurangzeb are typically pictured dripping with large spinel-bead
necklaces, engraved pendants or talismans, *bazubands,* and earrings made from simple
gold wire with a large spinel bead and an equally large pearl on either side.

The name spinel comes from the Latin word *spina,* meaning 'thorn', referring to the
sharp points of the octahedron, a common crystal habit of spinel, which consists
of eight triangular crystal faces. It has a hardness of 8 on the Mohs scale. Like ruby
and garnet, spinel has also been referred to as carbuncle, from the Latin *carbunculus,*
meaning 'small coal'.

In India, *lalri* (also called *suryamani,* gem of the sun) is used synonymously with spinel:
lal means 'red'. When the Hindi term *naram* is used, it denotes the balas ruby, which
we know today to be a misnomer.

Gold necklace set with spinel and turquoise
Uttar Pradesh, Lucknow
Nineteenth century

A three-strand gold necklace with floral-shaped links, hanging from triangular finials set with
a central cabochon spinel surrounded by turquoises. In the centre there are three gold
roundels, also set with a central cabochon spinel and surrounded by turquoises. Bunches of
pearls are attached to each roundel and each triangle.

This style of necklace is commonly worn by men in Uttar Pradesh as well as in Punjab.

Since ancient times, the royal treasuries of India have contained vast quantities of precious stones traded from Afghanistan, Sri Lanka and Burma. Sri Lanka was the principal source of sapphires and the Kingdom of Pegu (central Burma) became the source of rubies and spinel. Wealthy merchants from abroad travelled to the city of Ava, founded in 1364 as the capital of the Burmese Kingdom, to trade the precious stones.

Old Arabic writings refer to ruby/spinel mines in northern Afghanistan where, 'during the time of Abbaside (caliphate AD 750–1258), a hill at Chatlan was broken open by an earthquake and within a white rock in the fracture was found the ''Laal-Bedaschan'' or balas ruby.'[1] The Badakhshan mines were of great importance and the best quality stones were unearthed from mines along the Amu Darya, historically known by its Latin name Oxus, the river that separates present day Tajikistan and Uzbekistan from Afghanistan.

The thirteenth-century travelogue commonly called *The Travels of Marco Polo* or *Il Milione,* written down by Rustichello da Pisa from stories told by Marco Polo, describes Badkhshan as:

Bada[kh]shan is a Province inhabited by people who worship Mahommet…it is in this province that those fine and valuable gems the Balas Rubies are found…There is but one special mountain that produces them and it is called SYGHINAN…[2]

Spinel and rubies are found in the same deposits, and in the past there has been some confusion between the two minerals, but it is now clear that red spinel bears no resemblance to corundum, except that both minerals are oxides. Spinel is a magnesium-aluminium-oxide, whereas ruby is an aluminium-oxide. In the past, colour was the only criterion used for naming stones. There was also confusion with red garnet because of the colour resemblance to red spinel and ruby. When closely examined, spinel displays only one colour, while ruby gems commonly exhibit a slight to strong purplish red. Both red spinel and ruby often show strong red fluorescence in bright sunlight. Gem-quality red spinel was referred to as 'balas ruby', famous for its pink-to-deep-red variety that closely resembles ruby. The term 'balas' originally came from Balkh in Badakhshan.

Spinel is lighter in weight than ruby, and measures 8 on the Mohs scale, whereas ruby registers 9. It is also rare to find large gem-quality rubies, whereas large spinels are more common. The mineral is found in a variety of colours including purple, blue, dark green and black. The first red spinels to be mined were large—up to 500 carats. Because of their larger size and the custom of drilling precious stones, many were left uncut, but were often highly polished to bring out their true colour and subsequently drilled and used as beads. Only in 1783[3] were ruby and spinel distinguished on chemical grounds, but it was still easy to confuse rubies and red spinels; positive identification requires the use of optical or specific gravity/density tests.[4] It was not until the mid-nineteenth century that spinel was recognised as a separate mineral.

Only the finest early red spinels, appreciated for their soft-pink colour, size, lustre and translucency, were engraved with emperors' titles and/or texts. More recently, Mughal spinels with rulers' names and titles have appeared in collections, which indicates how much they were admired during the peak of the Mughal empire. Fine examples of these Badakhshan or balas rubies are found in some of the most famous gem collections in the world.

The Imperial State crown set with the Black Prince's Ruby
Royal Collection Trust/© Her Majesty Queen Elizabeth II 2017

Famous and Inscribed Spinels

Black Prince's Ruby

One of the finest examples of a Badakhshan spinel is the Black Prince's Ruby, an irregular bead-shaped spinel (approximately 170 carats) mounted above the Cullinan II diamond at the front of the Imperial State Crown, one of the oldest of the Crown Jewels of the United Kingdom. Its history dates back to the middle of the fourteenth century; it is said to have been worn by Edward, Prince of Wales, at the Battle of Crecy in the year 1346. Although referred to as a ruby for the past six hundred years, its specific gravity and distinctive crystallisation classify it definitely and irrefutably as a red spinel.[5]

Timur Ruby

Also known as *Khiraj-i-alam* and 'Tribute to the World', this spinel has a very distinguished history, clues to which can be derived from the stone itself. The various names and/or additional inscriptions of the great former Mughal, Persian and Afghan rulers attest to the history of a bygone era. Following the British annexation of the Punjab in 1849, it was presented to Queen Victoria in 1851 by the directors of the East India Company, in the form of a bead weighing approximately 352.5 carats, and was shown that same year at the Great Exhibition at Crystal Palace in London. In 1853 the Timur Ruby was mounted in a necklace by the London Jewellers R. & S. Garrard & Co., and is now in the British Royal Collection.

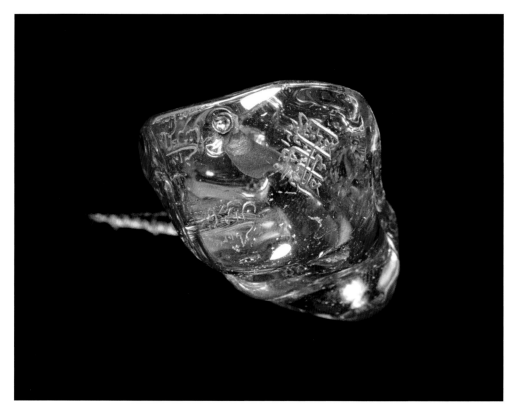

Carew Spinel

Another such irregular pear-shaped balas ruby is the famous Carew Spinel with
inscriptions engraved in Persian characters. The spinel was bequeathed to the Victoria
and Albert Museum in 1922 by the Rt Hon. Julia Mary, Lady Carew, who may have
been given it by the Aga Khan. This pear-shaped spinel has been drilled vertically and
set on a gold pin, with a diamond at the top and bottom. It weighs 133.5 carats, and
bears engraved inscriptions upon each of its four surfaces, the title and name of one
of four Mughal emperors: Akbar Shahi; Shah Akbar, Jahangir Shah 1021; Sahib Kiran
Sani 1039; Alamgir Shah 107(7) (in this case the last figure of the date is obscured or
may never have been engraved; only the figures 107 can be read with certainty).

Imperial Crown of Russia

The court jeweller and one of Russia's most celebrated diamond cutters, Jeremia
Pauzie, created the Imperial Crown of Russia (also known as the Great Imperial
Crown of Russia) for the coronation of Catherine the Great in 1762. It was used by
the emperors of Russia until the last coronation on 26 May 1896 for Nicholas II, the
final Tsar of Russia. The beautiful crown is adorned with 4,963 diamonds and one of
the seven historic stones of the Russian Diamond Collection. The world's second-
largest red spinel, set on top of the Imperial Crown, weighing 398.72 carats, had been
acquired nearly a century earlier in 1676, in Beijing, by Nicholas Spafary, the Russian
envoy to China from 1675 to 1678. The Imperial Crown of Russia is on display at the
Kremlin Armoury State Diamond Fund in Moscow.

Empress Nur Jahan

Nur Jahan

This spinel at the Chicago Field Museum of Natural History has the inscription
'*nur jahan*' ('light of the universe'). Nur Jahan (1577–1645), consort of the Mughal
Emperor Jahangir, was the most powerful and influential woman at court during
a period when the Mughal empire was at the peak of its power and glory. She is
considered by historians to have been the real power behind the throne for more
than fifteen years.

Samarian Spinel

The 500-carat Samarian spinel is said to be the largest gemstone of its kind and
is part of the Crown Jewels of Iran. The Royal Mace of Iran is a ceremonial mace
encrusted with spinels and diamonds; the largest of these spinels being the six
surrounding the top of the mace, each weighing 40 carats. The treasury is situated
inside the Central Bank of the Islamic Republic of Tehran.

The al-Sabah Collection

The collection of Sheikh Nasser Sabah al-Ahmad al-Sabah and his wife Sheikha
Hussah Sabah al-Salem al-Sabah, known as the al-Sabah Collection, holds the largest
royally inscribed spinels in the world, with the exception only of those held at the
National Jewels Treasury of Iran. Among them is a large spinel with the second-oldest
such inscription known to refer to Akbar, Jahangir and Shah Jahan.

1. Article excerpt from Halford-Watkins,
The Book of Ruby & Sapphire, pp.256–267.

2. Yule, *Il Milione*, Book 1, Chapter 29.

3. Meen and Tushingham, *Crown Jewels of Iran*,
p.32.

4. Keene, *The Lapidary Arts in Islam*.

5. Ménasché, *Ceylon: island of gems*, p.18.

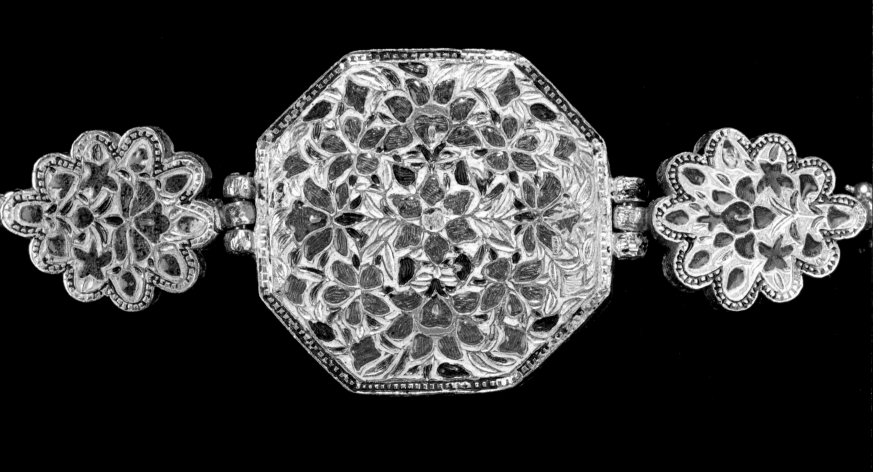

Nava Ratna

Harmony between Man and the Planets

The human body is described as an island with nine gems. It is believed that the nine gems protect nine parts of the human body: flesh, fat, bones, hair, feelings, marrow, lymph, blood and sperm; the number nine is considered to be a holy number.

In the science of Hindu astrology, the concept of Indian gemology is based on planetary influence and is said to yield fruitful results and changes for better living conditions. According to ancient Indian astrological wisdom, man is under the influence of the nine planets, represented by nine gems. Only Mercury, Venus, Mars, Jupiter and Saturn are recognised as planets, but there are also Rahu, the ascending node, and Ketu, the descending node, known in Hindu mythology as the 'shadow' planets. They are the points of intersection of the moon and sun's orbits. At the ascending node the moon moves from the southern half to the northern half of the sun's orbit; at the descending node the moon changes from the north to the south. With the sun, the moon, Rahu and Ketu and the five planets, Indian astrology has its nine planets, which are represented by nine gems. The Bhavanopanishad (which contains some of Hinduism's fundamental texts) describes the human body as an island with nine gems. The nine gems are thought to protect nine parts of the human body: flesh, fat, bones, hair, feelings, marrow, lymph, blood and sperm; the number nine is considered to be a holy number.

Octagonal gold armlet
Rajasthan, Bikaner
Late eighteenth century

An octagonal gold container-type *bazuband*, set with nine precious stones in the *nava ratna* arrangement (clockwise): ruby in the centre, surrounded by blue sapphire, topaz, diamond, emerald, zircon, pearl, coral and cat's eye in a rosette design, surrounded by cabochon rubies and turquoises. Two almond-shaped end pieces affixed on either side are also set with cabochon rubies and turquoises. All stones are set in the *kundan* technique.

The reverse is decorated with enamel in a floral motif on a gold surface in *champlevé* technique.

These octagonal box-type jewels sometimes held miniature Qur'ans and were worn on the upper arm as amulets. The nava ratna *arrangement of the stones provides further protection.*

Further information:
Babur's Heritage, p.77
Keene and Kaoukji, *Treasury of the World*, p.85, illustration 6.56 for a similar armlet(s)
Hasson, *Later Islamic Jewellery*, p.38, illustration 49

Nava ratna is a Sanskrit compound word meaning 'nine gemstones' (*nava* meaning 'nine' and *ratna* meaning 'gemstone').

There is a traditional mystical arrangement of these nine gemstones determined by rules known to astrologers and jewellers; ruby is always in the centre representing the sun as the centre of the solar system. The ruby is surrounded (clockwise) by: a diamond, a natural pearl, a red coral, a zircon (hyacinth, hessonite), a blue sapphire, a cat's eye, a topaz and an emerald. Before setting a gem in a jewel, the stones are taken to a priest for blessing and at an auspicious time the craftsman will start filling the order according to individual variations determined by the horoscopes. Jewellery set in this arrangement has important cultural significance in Hinduism, Jainism, Buddhism and Islam, the arrangement of the nine gems is used abundantly in India. In addition to India, great importance is also attached to this combination of nine gems in almost all countries in Asia; in Thailand the *nava ratna* is officially recognised as a national and royal symbol of the king.

In ancient Indian astrology each planet has a personality, a magnetic field and subtle vibrations, all of which influence life forces and human destiny. Because of their influence on each other, they are called *graha*. From a human point of view, planets are the most effective heavenly bodies; they are ruled by higher powers and are considered to be the celestial counterparts of man. They can influence mankind by giving it the fruits of their good and bad karma.

The nine gemstones are mythologically connected to the *nava grahas*, the nine celestial deities and their nine planets, each working in conjunction with their specific planet to keep the universe in harmony. According to Indian astrology, the planets, their associated deities and the nine gems are identified as follows:

Nava grahas	**Nine Astral Deities**	*Nava ratna*
Sun	Surya	Ruby
Venus	Shukra	Diamond
Moon	Chandra	Pearl
Mars	Mangal	Coral
Ascending node (Dragon's Head)	Rahu	Zircon (hyacinth, hessonite)
Saturn	Shani	Sapphire (blue)
Descending node (Dragon's Tail)	Ketu	Cat's eye
Jupiter	Brhaspati	Topaz
Mercury	Budha	Emerald

The *nava grahas* are worshipped all over India. In South India, their images are generally found in all important temples dedicated to Lord Shiva and they are always placed on a pedestal in a separate section of the temple, usually to the north-east of the *sanctum sanctorum*. Different temples install the *nava grahas* in different arrangements. In Indian astrology movement of the *nava grahas* is considered to influence the energy and mind of any individual connected to Earth, but humans are also capable of tuning themselves to the chosen energy of a specific *graha*.

Surya is the chief of the *nava grahas* who defers to the sun. He illuminates our planet and is therefore known as the eye of the universal being. The power that keeps him shining is regarded as the deity and he is an important element of Hindu astrology. The sun is the supreme symbol of all that is bright, he is the maker of the day, and also the centre of all cosmic forces. The white light which radiates from the sun is a combination of all the colours of the spectrum. These colours, in combination with the seven planets, are portrayed as a manifestation of the seven cosmic rays. Being the central celestial deity, he was worshipped all over ancient India in innumerable forms. In later icons he is often depicted riding a one-wheeled chariot and handling the reins of either four or seven mares, which are said to represent the seven colours of the rainbow or the seven chakras in the body. In other icons his chariot is drawn by a horse with seven heads.

Shukra, as the son of an astrologer, plays an important part in any horoscope. With his rich and varied personality, he is the creator of beauty and marital harmony, and plays the role of patron of magical arts and erotica. In his right hand he holds a rosary and in his left hand he carries a beggar's pot.

Chandra was born from the ocean when the gods decided to churn it in an attempt to find the elixir of life. He is the young and beautiful lunar deity, mostly two-armed and holding a club and a lotus in his hands. Every night he rides his chariot (the moon) through the sky, pulled by an antelope, or sometimes by ten white horses. All that is occult is governed by the moon, which is why he is called the mind of the universe, the one who sees the inner world.

Mangal is celibate and the god of violence and war, associated with Karttikeya. In the traditional order, the sun and moon are followed by Mangal. He is often depicted with four arms, riding a buffalo and his skin is usually red. In his hands he holds a trident, a sword and a mace and sometimes he holds a lotus in his fourth hand, or makes a gesture implying that Mars (Mangal) is not entirely bad and if well placed he can bestow you with peace and happiness. Sometimes Mangal is also depicted with two arms and holding lotus buds in both hands whilst riding a white ram or a chariot drawn by eight horses.

Shani, according to Indian mythology, is the son of Surya and his wife Chhaya (the shadow). Because he is the son of Chhaya, he is depicted as dark (black or blue) in colour and his clothes are black; he rides an iron chariot drawn by eight serpents although sometimes his chariot is pulled by crows, horses or eagles, or he is shown riding a buffalo. Shani has four hands, and holds a spear, an arrow and a bow, and makes a gesture of blessing with his fourth hand. Shani is very much worshipped in the south of India, where he is depicted with two hands, one holding an arrow and the other a rosary, and riding his chariot pulled by two ravens. It is very auspicious to go to the temple on a Saturday and offer his favourite items such as oil, black seeds and black cloth.

Brhaspati is known as the tutor of the gods. He is a beneficial planet, the bringer of peace and harmony to the world; his colour is yellow and/or gold and his divine attributes are a bow, arrows and a golden axe. As a symbol of aspiration to a higher spiritual life, he is seen riding a swan (*Hamsa*), but in some earlier images he is riding an elephant.

Budha is the son of Chandra or Soma (the moon) and Tara (the North Star), according to Indian mythology. He is handsome and has a greenish complexion. If Budha is accompanied by a malefic planet, then he too becomes malefic. He is shown with two hands holding a bow and a rosary and riding a lion. Sometimes he has four arms and holds a sword, shield and a mace in his hands while making the gesture of blessing with his right (fourth) hand. He rides his yali (a mythical animal with a lion's body and an elephant's head), wearing a king's robe.

The Story of Rahu and Ketu

Rahu is the mythical planet personified by the demon Rahu, disguised as a god, who tried to steal the nectar amrita (the potion of immortality), which had been extracted from the ocean while the gods were churning. The sun and the moon caught him in the act of stealing and reported this to Vishnu, who threw his discus towards Rahu, which cut off his head. The head, separated from the body, became immortal, as did the body. Vishnu flung both body parts into space, where the head became Rahu (Dragon's Head), the ascending node of the moon, and the body became Ketu (Dragon's Tail), the descending node of the moon. Rahu lives in the sky and races across the heavens in his silver chariot, pulled by eight black horses or lions, full of hatred for the sun and the moon. Occasionally, when he can, he swallows them, causing solar and lunar eclipses. In general Rahu is depicted as just a head, but sometimes he is seen with half a body and then he might have two or four arms, holding the moon in one of his hands.

Ketu is depicted as a human body without a head, with two arms, holding a sword and a lamp in his two hands. In some miniatures we see Ketu as a headless person with a fish-like tail. Ketu rides a chariot pulled by eight green horses.

In Hindu astrology each of the *grahas* can be associated with various characters and their attributes. This is subject to the interpretation, location and influences of the aspirations and needs of human society. In the oldest scriptures, the Rigveda, we learn about the one supreme spirit or god, called Brahma, who is shown in many different forms: male or female, human or animal, half human or half animal, as Indra, Lord of the Sky, as Agni, Lord of Fire, as Varuna, Lord of the Water. All these images are manifestations of the Vedic gods of whom Brahma, Vishnu and Shiva are the most important.

Because of the close relationship between man and the planets, *nava ratna* arrangements are found in many jewellery designs, such as floral motifs and bird forms, but the most common arrangement of the gems is in a circle or a square. It is believed that the use of *nava ratna* bestows longevity, health, wealth and progeny thereby assuring all-round happiness, also that it gives the wearer the will to liberate himself from the cycle of birth and death and to attain salvation. This philosophical background explains why *nava ratna* jewels are donated to temples as votive offerings and teaches us that jewellery in India is not only a symbol of luxury or social status, but also has a deep spiritual significance touching the innermost sublime feelings of devout people.

The traditional *nava ratna* arrangement for a square ring:[1]

Centre	Sun	Ruby
East	Venus	Diamond
South-east	Mercury	Emerald
South	Mars	Coral
South-west	Rahu (ascending node)	Zircon
West	Saturn	Sapphire
North-west	Ketu (descending node)	Cat's eye
North	Moon	Pearl
North-east	Jupiter	Topaz (white)

Gradually, influenced by the Mughals' penchant for arrangement, royals began to appreciate the beauty of the *nava ratna*. *Kundan*-set *meena* (enamelled) necklaces and chokers, with nine gems as the focus, became coveted pieces in every royal household. Artisans would source gems of the highest and best quality to design magnificent pieces, but only flawless stones in this arrangement can protect the wearer from evil influences and give him everything he desires. Second-rate stones are not strong enough to counterbalance the influence of the planets.

Scholars have written that Akbar (1556–1605), one of the greatest kings of all time, was deeply fond of the *nava ratna* design and owned many jewels, swords and daggers studded with the nine precious stones. At his court were nine distinguished courtiers acting as his closest advisers, popularly known as the *nava ratnas of Akbar*.

According to the Agastimata (an ancient book on gemstones), there are two distinct groups within the nine gems; the five greater and four lesser gems. The greater gems— diamond, pearl, sapphire, emerald and ruby—are called *maharatnani*, and are considered more precious and more powerful in terms of their healing and magical properties. The lesser gems—coral, zircon (hyacinth, hessonite), cat's eye and topaz—are called *uparatnani*. They may vary in their use, while the *maharatnani* are standardised. Since ancient times, Indian society has been organised on the basis of a scientific division of human activities. There was a priestly and intellectual class of Brahmins who gave advice on spiritual, political and religious matters. Members of this class were expected to be well versed in the scriptures and philosophical concepts to be able to transfer this knowledge to all members of society including royalty.

The *kshatriyas* were the warrior or defender class, who guarded the social structure against outside aggression. Kings usually fall into this category, when advised by the Brahmin. The *vaishyas* were traders and professionals in exchanging commodities. The *shudras*, the service class, were engaged in all kinds of manual work.

The nine gems correspond to the four categories because of their close relationship with, and influence on, human affairs.

1. For further information, see Pressmar, *Indian Rings*, p.25.

Gold pendant
West Bengal, Murshidabad
Late eighteenth century

length: 4.5 × 3.5 cm (total length 5.5 cm)

Gold oval pendant set with nine precious stones in the *nava ratna* arrangement. In the centre, a cabochon star ruby is surrounded by (clockwise): cat's eye, emerald, diamond, pearl, coral, topaz, blue sapphire and zircon. The precious stones are set in the *kundan* technique on a surface of monochrome (*partajikam*) *sabz zamin* (green enamel). The pendant is decorated with sixteen small cabochon rubies. On top are two loops with a flower decoration soldered to the pendant. Below are four hollow gold beads attached by gold wire through a loop soldered to the pendant.

On the reverse is an exquisitely enamelled floral and foliage pattern on a gold surface, with visible traces of white enamel bordering the central decoration. The side edge shows traces of green and red enamel.

Pendants were an important accessory during the Mughal period and often used as a vehicle to display the most valuable gems. Pendants composed of stones were worn for astrological reasons to increase the effect of a certain planet or to repel a malefic influence.

Pair of small bands
Uttar Pradesh, Benares (Varanasi)
Nineteenth century

Pair of small gold bands, *kundan*-set on a green-enamelled ground with the nine stones of the *nava ratna* arrangement: ruby, diamond, emerald, sapphire, coral, pearl, cat's eye, hyacinth and white topaz. The inner side of each band shows painted pink *gulabi* enamel with a pattern of lotus flowers on a translucent green ground which is typical for Benares.

Considering the sizes of the bands it is quite possible that the two bands might have belonged to the fineries of a costume doll or even a deity in the family shrine at home.

Pair *bazubands*
Uttar Pradesh, Lucknow
Nineteenth century

Pair of square gold *bazubands, kundan*-set with precious stones
according to the *nava ratna* arrangement (clockwise): white sapphire, emerald, diamond, pearl, coral, hessonite, blue sapphire, cat's
eye, with a cabochon ruby in the centre. A gold wire cord on
either side is attached to a flower-shaped hinge, *kundan*-set with
diamonds and emeralds. *Sabz zamin* (vegetable-green enamel)
decorates the reverse with some touches of light-blue enamel.

Bazubands *are worn on the upper arm.*

Further information:
Untracht, *Traditional Jewelry of India*, p.304, illustration 711

Gold *patri har*, long necklace, with pendant
Uttar Pradesh, Lucknow
Nineteenth century

length, without pendant: 26.5 cm
pendant: 8 x 5 cm

Gold *patri har* (long necklace) with pendant, consisting of two sets of nine square units, strung in five strands and separated by five small irregular pearls. The eighteen gold units (nine mirror images) are all polychrome enamelled with images depicting the nine *nava grahas* (astral deities) with their mounts. The square units are each *kundan*-set with a diamond on each of the four corners.

On the reverse, the eighteen gold units are polychrome enamelled with a white enamel outline (*safed chalwan*) around various birds, such as peacocks and parrots, and floral themes.

Front
Pendant in the style of a single flower on a stem with a carved cabochon ruby in the centre, surrounded by twelve diamonds which, in turn, are surrounded by nine smaller diamonds, eight small emeralds and eight small rubies. The outer edge is decorated with nine gems in the *nava ratna* arrangement: ruby in the centre, followed by (clockwise) diamond, pearl, coral, hessonite, cat's eye, blue sapphire, yellow sapphire and emerald, alternated with smaller gemstones in the same arrangement.

All stones are set in the *kundan* technique

The pendant has a pearl on top and a suspended spinel bead.

Reverse

The reverse of the pendant depicts a polychrome enamelled image of Lord Shiva, the third god of the Hindu triad. He sits on a yellow-enamelled tiger skin, symbolising that he is the source of all creative energy and is above and beyond any kind of force. He supports the celestial river Ganga in his long brown hair. Lord Shiva is decorated with coiled snakes (nagas) around his neck, shoulders and on top of his matted hair and he wears three necklaces as well as *bazubands* (upper armlets) and bangles on both wrists.

This image shows Lord Shiva with *vibhuti*, three lines of ashes drawn on the forehead, signifying the Immortality of the Lord and his manifested glory

On this pendant Lord Shiva is painted blue due to having drunk poison during the time of the churning of the ocean by the gods.

Front of gold units, detail

1. The black-enamelled Rahu is depicted in front of the white-enamelled moon, in his silver chariot. The chariot is driven by a charioteer dressed in golden yellow, and pulled by a light-blue-enamelled horse. The background is red-enamelled. The unit is decorated with seven *kundan*-set diamonds.

9. Surya (the Sun), dressed completely in white, wears a crown on his head. He rides his one-wheeled chariot pulled by seven white-enamelled horses and driven by a charioteer dressed in yellow gold with a crown on his head.

The background is red-enamelled and he is surrounded by seven *kundan*-set diamonds.

Further information:
Untracht, *Traditional Jewelry of India*, p.311, illustration 317 (detail)

2. Mangal (Mars) is depicted with orange-enamelled skin and clothes and four arms, riding a white-enamelled ram covered with a green-checked-enamelled cloth. He is surrounded by white-enamelled lotus flowers and light-blue-enamelled leaves, on a red-enamelled background, with a *kundan*-set diamond in each corner.

3. Ketu is depicted, as a human body without a head, with a black-checked-enamelled fish-like tail. Ketu is shown here with four arms and three attributes, in his lower left hand he holds a victory banner; his upper left hand displays a shield, and in his lower right hand he holds a lasso. On his right and left sides are white-enamelled lotus flowers on a red-enamelled background with a *kundan*-set diamond in each corner.

4. Bhuda (Mercury) is depicted with a white-enamelled body and four arms; he wears a king's costume and a crown. He rides a *yali* (a mythical animal with a lion's body and an elephant's head). His mount is covered with a yellow-enamelled cloth, and he is surrounded by green-enamelled plants on a red-enamelled background with a *kundan*-set diamond in each corner.

5. Chandra (the moon) is depicted wearing a white dupatta and a white loincloth; he has four arms and holds a lotus in his upper right hand and a club in his upper left hand. He rides a black-enamelled antelope. He is surrounded by green plants on a red-enamelled background with a *kundan*-set diamond in each corner.

6. Shukra (Venus), wearing a green- and gold-enamelled dupatta and an yellow-enamelled loincloth. He has four arms and rides a black-enamelled horse, which is covered with a light-blue-enamelled cloth with gold-enamelled dots. The background is red-enamelled with a *kundan*-set diamond in each corner.

7. Brhaspati (Jupiter) is dressed in a yellow- or gold-enamelled dupatta and loincloth. He has four arms and holds a stick in his lower left hand. He rides a black-enamelled elephant. The background is red-enamelled, and features a branch with white and light-blue enamel leaves on each side of the elephant. There is a *kundan*-set diamond in each corner.

8. Shani (Saturn), dressed completely in black, wears a crown on his head. He has four arms and rides a buffalo, which is covered with a green-checked-enamelled cloth. The background is red-enamelled with some branches of white-enamelled lotus flowers and light-blue-enamelled leaves and a *kundan*-set diamond in each corner.

Reverse of gold units, detail

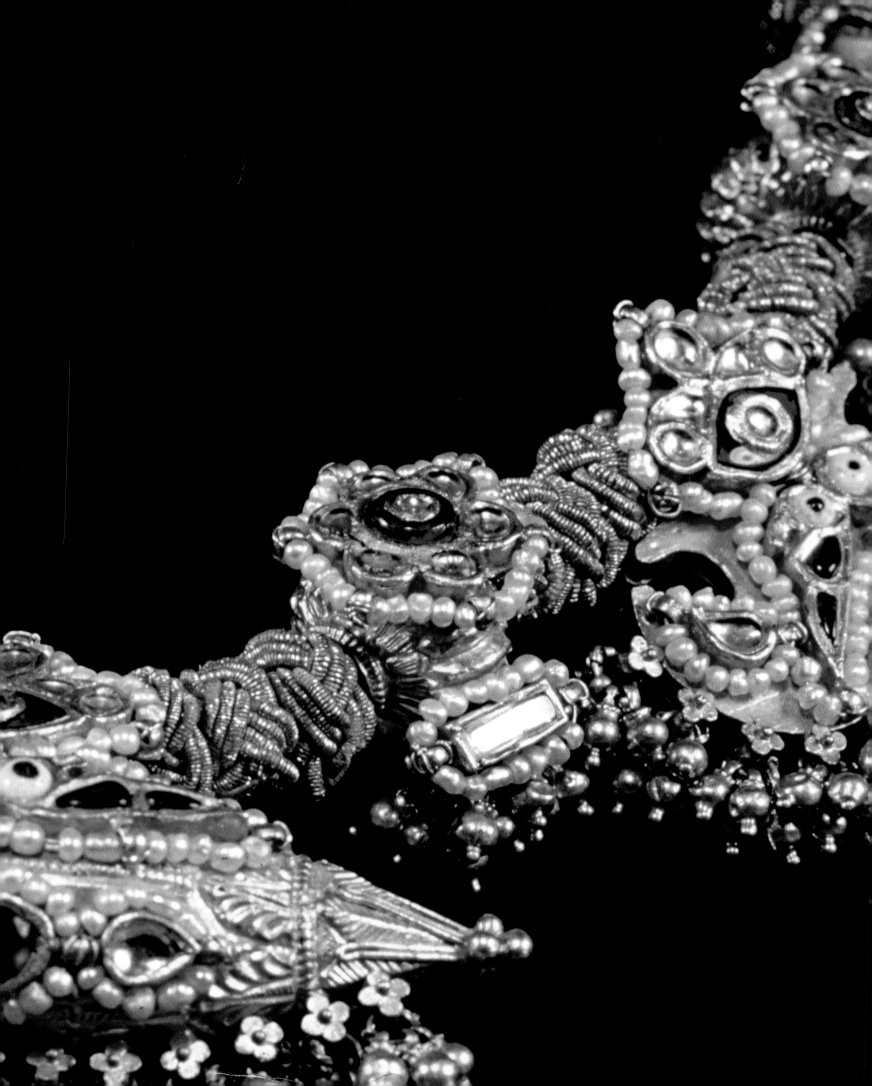

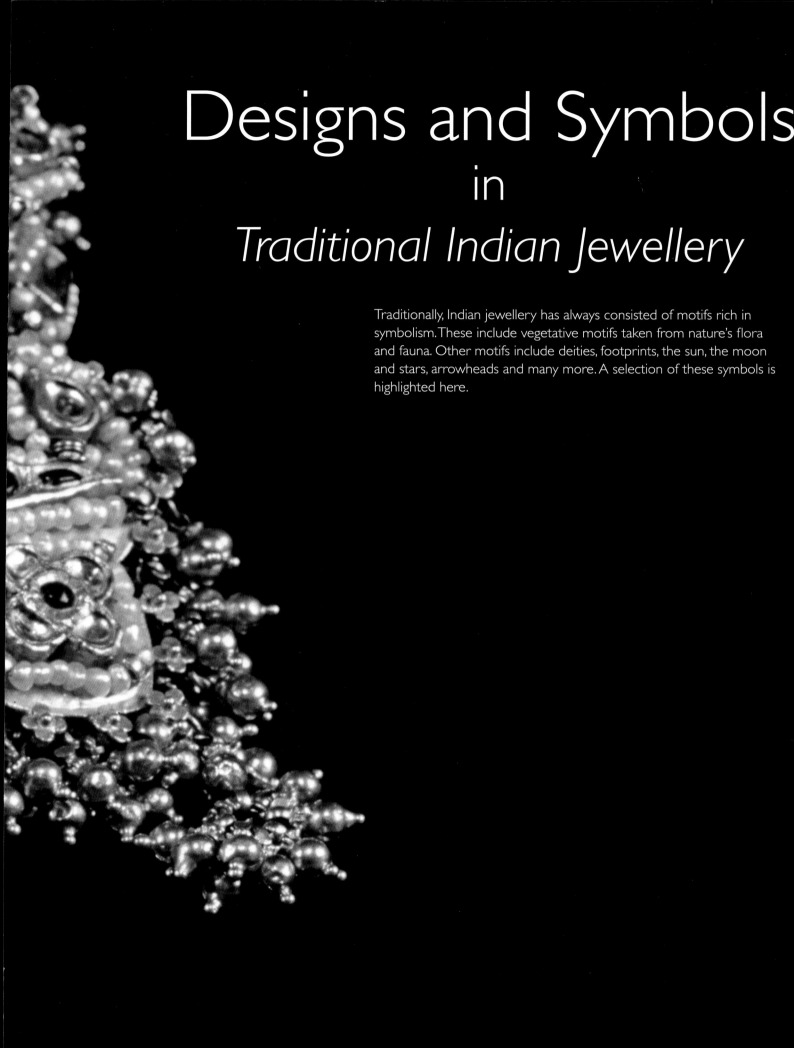

Designs and Symbols
in
Traditional Indian Jewellery

Traditionally, Indian jewellery has always consisted of motifs rich in symbolism. These include vegetative motifs taken from nature's flora and fauna. Other motifs include deities, footprints, the sun, the moon and stars, arrowheads and many more. A selection of these symbols is highlighted here.

Sun

The sun is the supreme solar motif and is regarded as the source of all life on Earth.

Gold symbolises the warmth of the sun.

Crescent Moon

An emblem of peace and calm, the moon symbolises the Great Divine Mother (known as Shakti) and female power.

Silver symbolises the coolness of the moon.

Sun with Crescent Moon

Within the tradition of bridal decoration in South India, there are several pieces of jewellery worn on the head, starting with the elaborate *thalaisaamaan*—one part rests on the forehead, below the centre parting of the hair and is held in place by two matching jewels worn on either side of the brow at the hairline. On top of the head, on either side, the *suryabottu* (the sun) represents male strength, and the *chandrabott* (the crescent moon) represents Shakti; together they are called *jadapillai*. These are followed by a third decoration that represents the *thazhambu* (a fragrant screwpine flower).

Arrowhead

The arrowhead has had great symbolic meaning since ancient times; it was believed to possess the power to destroy the evil in the world. To obtain this protection, a pendant in the form of an arrowhead was worn around the neck. Eventually, the simple arrowhead evolved into a more stylised and embellished form; additional decorations reinforce the amulet's auspicious power.

Floral Designs

The depiction of flowers in Indian jewellery has been passed down from time immemorial.

The **lotus** (*padma*), the national flower of India, sprouts in muddy water and unfolds itself into a beautiful flower while resting on, but not touching, the surface of the water. At night the flower closes and sinks beneath the water, rising and opening again at dawn. It is the symbol of purity and rebirth.

The lotus is associated with spirituality in both Hinduism and Buddhism. Many Hindu deities are shown sitting or standing on a large open lotus pedestal, which is a symbol of support for those who represent the highest transcendental essence. The symbol of the lotus pedestal denotes divine physical life. Numerous deities are shown carrying lotus rosettes or lotus buds in their hands. In Indian mythology, the goddess Sarasvati is depicted seated on a white lotus.

The goddess Lakshmi is considered to be the lotus goddess with lotus eyes (*padmaksi*), and is often described as *padmasambhava* (lotus-born), and represented as *padmesthita* (standing on a lotus pedestal) or depicted sitting on a pink lotus, bedecked with *padmamalini* (lotus garlands). The lotus rises from Vishnu's navel and is the seat of Brahma, the creator.

Bell-shaped earrings with smaller bells hanging within them, represent the lotus flower.

The lotus is prevalent in Indian, Chinese and Japanese decoration, as well as on Assyrian and Babylonian sculptures.

The *Michelia champaca* is a large evergreen exotic tree, known for its highly fragrant yellow or white flowers. In India, girls and women wear the flowers in their hair as an ornament of beauty as well as a natural perfume.

Champa or frangipani flowers are often used for worship and as offerings to deities in shrines and temples. Champa flower buds have become an often-used motif in Indian jewellery design. *Champakali* necklaces consist of identical hanging units representing buds of the champa flower. According to legend, Buddha was born under a very tall champa tree.

The *Papaver somniferum* (**Opium poppy**) flower, with its lobed leaves, has often inspired enamellers and is regularly seen in their designs.

Leaf borders and scroll motifs have been used extensively in the artistry of jewellery design.

Rudraksha (*Elaeocarpus ganitrus*) is a medium-sized tree with a dense crown of foliage and an approximately conical form. The seeds from the fruit of the rudraksha tree are used as beads. The masses of white and sometimes pinkish flowers, with an unusual liquorice scent, hang downwards with cup-shaped feathery petals and fringed edges; the flowers are followed by shiny cobalt-blue fruit. Since the rudraksha tree favours a low-temperature and pollution-free environment, it grows abundantly in the hilly regions of Himachal Pradesh and Nepal.

Seeds from the fruit (called rudraksha) are classified into four categories according to their shape and size. *Rudra* means 'Shiva' in Sanskrit, and *aksha* means 'eye' in Sanskrit ('the eye of Shiva').

A Hindu legend tells us that Rudra, the fierce form of Shiva, burst into tears when he saw all the sorrow of mankind and there, where his first tear fell, the very first rudraksha tree germinated and grew.

Sometimes a *rudraksha* seed may have as many as fourteen mouths (*mukhas*), compartments that divide the seed.

The number of *mukhas* determines the spiritual effect. The common seed has five *mukhas*, which symbolises the five faces of Lord Shiva. Those having one to four or six to fourteen are the most rare.

Generally, the seeds are in four colours: white, red, yellow (goldish) and brown. Their superiority is based on the four Varnas, white being suggestive of Brahmin, red of Kshatriya, gold of Vaisya, and brown of Sudras. The rudraksha seeds should be worn on a black or red cord, and are only rarely seen on a gold chain. Hindus, Sikhs and Buddhists have considered the brown rudraksha beads to be one of the most sacred objects since at least the tenth century and holy men all over India wear the beads, usually around the neck and arms. During meditation strings of rudraksha beads are held in the hands.

For Hindus, the **tree of life** symbolises a cosmic tree that supports the whole universe and preserves all life. For Muslims, it is the tree that grew in the Garden of Paradise. It also represents immortality.

Fruits

The luscious juicy fruits growing abundantly all over India are a popular motif in all crafted objects, but they feature most extensively in jewellery design. The popular story often narrated suggests that God, in one of his creative provocations, extracted the juice from a mango tree and used it to paint the figure of a woman who looked so beautiful that she outshone even the *apsaras* (celestial nymphs).

Mango always appears in a stylised form and is reproduced as an asymmetrical ornament. It is a symbol of happiness, a prosperous future and satisfaction, love and fertility.

Birds

Birds and animals that have mythological associations are often used in Indian jewellery and works of art.

Of all the birds, the **peacock** is the most important, not only because of its beauty, elegance and colourful body and features, but also as the *vahana* (mount) of Shiva and Paravati's second son, Skanda, also known as Kumara or Karttikeya. The graceful peacock, with its iridescent feathers, is admired all over India; it is often seen depicted with a floriated tail. This has been a particular feature of Indian art since very ancient times and is mentioned in ancient Sanskrit literary works. Peacocks symbolise joy, beauty and pride, and it is believed they can kill serpents.

As the *vahana* (mount) of Kamadeva, son of Vishnu and Lakshmi, the **parrot** is the god of human love, desire and passion, and also of fertility. The parrot is also a symbol of knowledge and learning.

As the *vahana* of Brahma (creator of the universe), as well as the goddess Saraswathi, Hamsa (the **swan**) typifies grace and beauty, symbolises logical thought, and the knowledge of the difference between right and wrong, while the beauty and purity of his white feathers signifies auspiciousness. It is also believed that Hamsa has the ability to separate water from milk, spitting out the water

then drinking the milk. Similarly, it is believed that the evolved human being should separate good from evil.

Hamsa often features in *rakodi*, a hair ornament forming part of a South Indian head decoration.

Animals

Associated with Indra, Lord of the Celestial World, whose *vahana* is the white elephant, Airavat, **elephants** symbolise kingship and they flank entrances to royal palaces.

The Hindu Puranas suggest that elephants in the past had wings and that Airavat emerged during the churning of the ocean by the gods and demons. In Hindu India, a **white horse** is a symbol of the sun associated with Surya; its head represents knowledge. In the Vedic tradition, horses symbolise speed, beauty and purity.

The goddess Lakshmi, in one of her innumerable forms, is sometimes flanked by **deer**, which symbolise love and beauty.

Considered throughout India to be holy, and a symbol of purity and *ahimsa* (non-violence), the **cow** is the living symbol of Mother Earth. Kamadhenu, the celestial cow, is considered the mother of all cows, representing abundance and sacrifice.

The *vahana* of the Hindu god Shiva is a **bull**, Nandi (meaning 'giving delight'), the symbol of his lord's divine nature. Nandi is often shown in a sitting position at the entrance to Shiva temples. He is symbolic of eternal waiting, hence waiting is a form of meditation and therefore considered the greatest virtue in Indian life.

The **cobra** symbolises peace and calm. It is a well-known fact that they never attack unless provoked. As a symbol of fertility, snakes were venerated for the birth of a son. The snake primarily represents rebirth, due to its ability to cast its skin and to be symbolically reborn. Nagas play an important role in many legends and snake worship refers to the high status of snakes in Hindu mythology. The serpent Shesh Naga with a thousand heads, is the couch and canopy of Lord Vishnu while sleeping during the intervals in creation. Sometimes Shesh Naga is portrayed supporting the world and sometimes holding the seven hells. It is believed that whenever Shesh Naga yawns he causes earthquakes. Shesh Naga is also called Ananta (endless), as a symbol of eternity, and is used as a braid ornament in South India, known as *jadanaagam*.

The first avatar of Lord Vishnu, according to the Hindu theory of evolution, the **fish** was the first creature to be born in the waters. The fish symbol is used extensively in traditional Indian jewellery, especially in ear ornaments and pendants.

Kurma is the second avatar of Lord Vishnu, who took the form of a giant **turtle** to support Mandara during the churning of the ocean.

Makara is a mythical aquatic animal with the head of a crocodile and the tail of a fish, and is the *vahana* of Varuna, Lord of the Waters, and also of the two great river goddesses, Ganga and Yamuna.

Gods and Goddesses

Temple jewellery is jewellery given as an offering in the temple and used to adorn the idols of gods and goddesses. Lots of jewellery such as pendants, bangles and necklaces depicting deities are worn all over the subcontinent.

Vishnupada, the footprints of Lord Vishnu, are considered sacred by Hindus. Vishnupada may be carved in stone or formed in gold or silver, and may show symbols referring to specific deities.

Vishnu, the preserver, is one of the three gods in the great Hindu trinity, the other two being Brahma, the creator, and Shiva, the destroyer.

Bibliography

Abu'l-Fazl 'Allami. *Akbar-Nama, of Abu'L-Fazl*, trans. H. Beveridge. London; Low Price Publication, New Delhi, 2013.

Aitken, M.E. *When Gold Blossoms. Indian jewelry from the Susan L. Beningson Collection*. Asia Society and Philip Wilson, New York, 2004. Exhibition catalogue.

Amina, Okada. *L'inde des Princes*. Réunion des musées nationaux, Paris, 2000.

Archer, Mildred. *Company Paintings: Indian paintings of the British period*. Victoria and Albert Museum, London, 1992.

Archer, Mildred, Christopher Rowell and Robert Skelton. *Treasures from India: the Clive Collection at Powis Castle*. Herbert Press/National Trust, London, 1987.

Aryan, Subhashini. *Crafts of Himachal Pradesh*. Mapin Publishing, Ahmedabad, 1993.

Aziz, Abdul. *The Imperial Treasury of the Indian Mughuls,* Vols I, II. Cosmo Publications, New Delhi, 2009.

Babur's Heritage: the influence of Mughal jewellery, ed. Bernadette van Gelder. Antwerp Diamond Museum, Antwerp, 2006. Exhibition catalogue.

Bala Krishnan, U. R. B. *Jewels of the Nizams*. India Book House, New Delhi, 2001.

Bala Krishnan, U. R. and M. S. Kumar. *Dance of the Peacock: jewellery traditions of India*. India Book House, New Delhi, 1999.

Bala Krishnan, Usha R., Oppi Untracht and Cecilia Levin. *Icons in Gold: jewelry of India from the collection of the Musée Barbier – Mueller*. Somogy Editions D'Art, Paris, 2005.

Balfour, Ian. *Famous Diamonds*, 4th edition. ACC Publishing, Woodbridge, UK, 2000.

Barnard, Nicholas. *Arts and Crafts of India*. Conran Octopus, London, 1993.

Barnard, Nick. *Indian Jewellery*. V&A Publishing, London, 2008.

Barriault, Anne B. and Rosalie A. West, eds. *The Arts of India*. Virginia Museum of Fine Arts, Virginia, 2001.

Begley, W. E. and Z. A. Desai. *Taj Mahal: the illuminated tomb*. The University of Washington Press, Seattle, 1989.

Begley, Wayne Edison and Ziyaud-Din A. Desai, eds. *The Shah Jahan Nama of Inayat Khan*. Oxford University Press, Delhi, 1990.

Bennet, David and Daniela Mascetti. *Understanding Jewellery*. ACC Publishing, Woodbridge, UK, 1994.

Bernier, François. *Travels in the Mogul Empire 1656-1668*. A Revised and Improved Edition based upon Irvin Brock's translation. Asian Educational Service, New Delhi, 1996.

Bhandari, Vandana. *Costume, Textiles and Jewellery of India: traditions in Rajasthan*. Mercury Books, San Diego, 2004.

Bharadwaj, Monisha. *Great Diamonds of India*. India Book House, Mumbai, 2002.

Birdwood, George Christopher Molesworth, Sir. *The Industrial Art of India*. Digitised by the Internet Archive, 2007.

Biswas, Arun Kumar and Sulekha Biswas. *Minerals and Metals in Ancient India*. D.K. Printworld, New Delhi, India, 1996.

Brijbhushan, Jamila. *Indian Jewellery Ornaments and Decorative Designs*, 2nd edition. D.B. Taraporevala, Maharastra, India, 1964.

Brijbhushan, Jamila. *Masterpieces of Indian Jewellery*. D.B. Taraporevala, Maharastra, India, 1979.

Bromberg, Anne R. *The Arts of India, Southeast Asia, and the Himalayas*. Dallas Museum of Art, 2013.

Brunel, Francis. *Jewellery of India: five thousand years of tradition*. National Book Trust, New Delhi, 1972.

Calouste Gulbenkian Foundation. *Vasco da Gama and India*. Vol. 1 Political and military history. International Conference, Paris, 11–13 May 1998. Fundacoa Calouste Gulbekian, Lisboa, 1999.

Carvalho, Pedro Moura, Henrietta Sharp and Stephen Vernoit. *Gems and Jewels of Mughal India*. Nour Foundation in association with Azimuth Editions, London, 2010. Exhibition catalogue.

Chauhan, Sumi Krishna. *Delhi, Agra & Jaipur: the golden triangle*. Tiger Books, London, 1988.

Chawla, Rupika. *Raja Ravi Varma: painter of colonial India*. Mapin Publishing, Ahmedabad, 2010.

Coomaraswamy, Ananda K. *The Arts & Crafts of India & Ceylon*. T. N. Foulis, London, 1913.

Coomaraswamy, Ananda Kentish. *The Wisdom of Ananda Coomaraswamy, Reflections on Indian art, life and religion*, ed. S. Durai Raja Singam and Joseph A. Fitzgerald. World Wisdom, Bloomington, Indiana, 2011.

Cooper, I. and J. Gillow. *Arts and Crafts of India*. Thames & Hudson, London, 1996.

Corrigan, Karina H., Jan van Campen, Femke Diercks and Janet C. Blyberg, eds. *Asia in Amsterdam: the culture of luxury in the Golden Age*. Rijksmuseum, Amsterdam, 2015. Exhibition catalogue.

Crespo, Hugo Miquel. *Joias da Carreira da India*. Museu do Oriente, Lisboa, 2014. Exhibition catalogue.

Crosby Forbes, H. A. *Chinese Export Silver 1785 to 1885,* The Stinehour Press, Lunenburg, Vermont, 1975.

Crosby Forbes, H. A., John Devereux Kernan and Ruth S. Wilkins. *Chinese Export Silver 1785 to 1885*. Museum of the American China Trade, Milton, Massachusetts, 1975.

Dalrymple, W. *White Mughals: love and betrayal in eighteenth-century India*. Penguin Books, London, 2002.

Dalrymple, William. *The Last Mughal: the fall of a dynasty*. Viking, Delhi, 2006.

Dautremer, Joseph. *Burma under British Rule – and Before*, trans. Sir James George Scott K.C.I.E. Charles Scribner, New York; T. Fisher Unwin, London, 1913.

Derek, J., ed. *The Pearl and the Dragon: a study of Vietnamese pearls and a history of the oriental pearl trade*. Houlton, Maine, 1999.

Dikshit, Moreshwar G., Dr. *History of Indian Glass*. University of Bombay, Bombay, 1969.

Doshi, Saryu, ed. *Pageant of Indian Art: Festival of India in Great Britain*. Marg Publications, Bombay, 1983.

Doshi, Saryu, Dr. *The Impulse to Adorn*. Marg Publications, Bombay, 1982.

Dunbar, George, Sir. *A History of India: from the earliest times to nineteen thirty-nine*. Nicholson & Watson, London, 1949.

Dunbar, George, Sir. *A History of India from the Earliest Times to The Present Day*. Nicholson & Watson, London, 1943.

Durlabhji, Rashmikant. *The Emerald Book*. Publication on behalf of Jaipur Jewellery Show, 2006.

Eden, Emily. *Up the Country: letters written to her sister from the upper provinces of India*. Cambridge Library Collection, Cambridge, 2010.

Estate of Jacqueline Kennedy Onassis. Sotheby's catalogue, New York, 1996.

Father Sangermano, *The Burmese Empire a Hundred Years Ago*, White Orchid Press, Hong Kong, 1995.

Foster, William, Sir, ed. *The Embassy of Sir Thomas Roe to the Court of the Great Mogul 1615-1619*. Editions Indian, Calcutta, 1965–66.

Gabriel, Hannelore. *The Jewelery of Nepal*. Weatherhill, New York, 1999.

Ganguly, Waltraud. *Earrings, Ornamental Identity and Beauty in India*. B.R. Publishing, New Delhi, 2007.

Ganguly, Waltraud. *Nose Rings of India*. B.R. Publishing, New Delhi, 2015.

Gans, M. H. *Juwelen en Mensen*. Interbook, J.H. de Bussy, University of California, 1979.

Gascoigne, B. *The Great Moghuls*. Harper & Row, London, 1971.

Gode, P. K. 'The Antiquity of the Hindoo Nose-Ornament called "Nath"', *Annals of the Bhandarkar Oriental Research Institute* XIX (1939): 313–334.

Gonda, Jan. 'The Functions and Significance of Gold in the Veda', *Orientalia Rheno-Traiectina* 37 (1991).

Goswamy, B. N. *Piety and Splendour: Sikh heritage in art*. National Museum, New Delhi, 2000.

Grimaldi, David A. *Amber Window to the Past*. Harry N. Abrams, New York, 1996.

Guiliani, Gaston, Marc Chaussidon, Henri-Jean Schubnel, Daniel H. Piat, Claire Rollion-Bard, Christian France-Lanord, Didier Giard, Daniel de Narvaez and Benjamin Rondeau. 'Oxygen Isotopes and Emerald Trade Routes Since Antiquities', *Science* 287 (2000).

Haafner, Jacob Gottfried. *Exotische Liefde*, ed. Thomas Rosenboom. Atheneum, Amsterdam, 2011.

Hackenbroch, Yvonne. *Renaissance Jewellery,* 1st edition. Sotheby Parke Bernet, New York, 1979.

Haidar, Navina Najat and Marika Sardar. *Sultans of Deccan 1500 – 1700: opulence and fantasy*. The Metropolitain Museum of Art, New York, 2015.

Halford-Watkins, J. F. The Book of Ruby & Sapphire from an unpublished 1936 manuscript, edited by Richard W. Hughes.

Hasson, Rachel. *Early Islamic Jewellery*. The L.A. Mayer Institute of Islamic Art, Jerusalem, 1987.

Hasson, Rachel. *Later Islamic Jewellery*. The L.A. Mayer Institute of Islamic Art, Jerusalem, 1987.

Hendley, T. Holbein. *C.I.E. Handbook to the Jeypore Museum*. Royal College of Surgeons of England.

Hendley, Thomas Holbein. *Indian Jewellery*. BR Publishing, Delhi, 2009.

Hendley, Thomas Holbein. *Memorials of the Jeypore Exhibition. Volume I: Industrial art 1883*. Exhibition catalogue.

Hendley, Thomas Holbein. *The Rulers of India and Chiefs of Rajputana, 1550-1897*. W. Griggs, London, 1897.

Hermitage Museum. *Catherine the Great*. Hermitage Museum, Amsterdam, 2016. Exhibition catalogue.

Hobsbawm, Eric and Terence Ranger, eds. *The Invention of Tradition* Cambridge University Press, Cambridge, 1983.

Hooja, Rima. *A History of Rajasthan*. Rupa Publications, New Delhi, 2006.

India: Jewels that enchanted the world. Kremlin Museums and Indo-Russian Foundation Publishing, 2014. Exhibition catalogue.

Jacob, S. S. and Thomas Holbein, Hendley. *Jeypore Enamels*. W. Griggs, London, 1886.

Jafa, Jyoti. *Nur Jahan*. Roli Books, New Delhi, 1994.

Jaffer, A., ed. *Beyond Extravagance: a royal collection of gems and jewels*. Assoulline, New York, 2013.

Jain, Jyotindra. *Folk Art and Culture of Gujarat: guide to the collection of the Shreyas Folk Museum of Gujarat*. Published by Shreyas Prakashan on behalf of the Shreyas Folk Museum of Gujarat, Ahmedabad, 1980.

Jain-Neubauer, Jutta, *Chandrika Silver Ornaments of India*. Timeless Books Kootenay, Canada, 2001.

Jain-Neubauer, Jutta. *Feet and Footwear in Indian Culture*. Grantha, London, 2000.

Jaques, Susan. *The Empress of Art: Catherine the Great and the transformation of Russia*. Pegasus Books, New York, 2016.

Jenkins, Marilyn and Manuel Keene. *Islamic Jewelry in the Metropolitan Museum of Art*. Metropolitan Museum of Art, New York, 1982.

Joyce, Kristin and Shellei Addison. *Pearls, Ornament and Obsession,* 1st edition. Simon & Schuster, New York, 1992.

Kanitkar, V. P. (Hemant) *Hinduism: religions of the world*. Franklin Watts London, 1986.

Keene, Manuel. 'The Lapidary Arts of Islam: an underappreciated tradition', *Expedition Magazine* 24 (1981).

Keene, Manuel and Salam Kaoukji. *Treasury of the World: jewelled arts of India in the age of the mughals*. The al-Sabah Collection, Kuwait National Museum, London, 2001. Exhibition catalogue.

Khalidi, Omar. *Romance of the Golconda Diamonds*. Mapin Publishing, Ahmedabad, 1999.

Krishna, Nanditha. *Arts and Crafts of Tamil Nadu*. Mapin, Ahmedabad, India, 1992.

Kunz, George Frederick. *The Curious Lore of Precious Stones*. Bell Publishing Company, New York, 1989.

Latif, Momin (part 1). *A Kaleidoscope of Colours: Indian Mughal jewels from the 18th and 19th centuries*. Antwerp Diamond Museum, Antwerp, 1997. Exhibition catalogue.

Latif, Momin. *Mughal Jewels*. Société Generale de Banque and Musée Royaux d'Art et d'Histoire, Brussels, 1982. Exhibition catalogue.

Losty, J. P. and Malini Roy. *Mughal India: art, culture and empire*. British Library, London, 2012.

Mannucci, Niccolao, *Storia do Mogor or Mogul India, 1653-1708*, trans. William Irvine. London, 1907. Reprinted New Delhi, 1981.

Markel, Stephen. *India's Fabled City: the art of courtly Lucknow*, Prestel Publishing and Los Angeles County Museum of Art, Munchen, London, New York, Los Angeles, 2010.

Mathur, AshaRani. *A Jewelled Splendor: the tradition of Indian jewellery*. Rupa Publications, Kolkota, India, 2002.

Mathur, AshaRani. *Diamond: Eternal Fire. The Indian diamond tradition*. Rupa Publications, Kolkota, India, 2006.

Matlins, Antoinette L. *The Pearl Book*. GemStone Press, Nashville, 1996.

Mazloum, Claude. *Jewellery and Gemstones*. Gremese International, Roma, 1990.

Meen, Victor Ben and Arlotte Douglas Tushingham. *Crown Jewels of Iran*. University of Toronto Press, Toronto, 1968.

Ménasché, Elie L. *Ceylon: island of gems*. Asian Educational Services, New Delhi, 1954.

Munn, Geoffrey C. *Castellani and Guiliano Revivalsist Jewellers of the Nineteenth Century*, 1st edition. Rizzoli, London, 1984.

Murthy, K. Krishna. *Mythical Animals in Indian Art*. Abhinav Publications, Maharastra, India, 1985.

Museu Nacional de Arte Antiga. *Esplendores do Oriente. Joias de Ouro da Antiga Goa*. Museu Nacional de Arte Antiga, Lisbon, 2014.

Nath, Aman and Francis Wacziarg, eds. *The Arts and Crafts of Rajasthan*. Thames & Hudson, London, 1987.

Nayeem, M.A. *The Splendour of Hyderabad*. Hyderabad Publishers, Hyderabad, 2002.

Nevile, Pran. *Nautch Girls of India*. Ravi Kumar, Paris, New York, New Delhi and Prakriti India, New Delhi, 1996.

Nevile, Pran. *Nautch Girls of India: dancers, singers, playmates*. Distributed by Variety Book Depot, New Delhi, 1996.

Nigam, M. L. *Indian Jewellery*. South Asia Books, New Delhi, 1999.

Okada, Amina. *L'Inde des Princes. La donation Jean et Krishna Riboud*. Musée des arts asiatiques, Guimet, 2000. Catalogue.

Pal, Pratapaditya, Janice Leoshko, Joseph M. Dye III and Stephen Markel. *Romance of the Taj Mahal*. Thames & Hudson, London, 1989.

Patel, Hansdev, Dr. *Royal Families and Palaces of Gujarat*. Scorpion Cavendish, London, 1998.

Pressmar, Emma. *Indian Rings*. New Order Book Co., Frankfurt, 1982.

Prior, K. and J. Adamson. *Maharajas' Jewels*. Vendome Press, New York, 2000.

Purchas, Samual. *Hakluytys Posthumus, or Purchas his Pilgrimes*. Cambridge University Press, Cambridge, 2014.

Ramnarine, R. *Some Concepts of Hinduism: an introduction*. Dr R. Ramnarine, 1997.

Randhawa, T. S. *The Last Wanderers: nomads and gypsies of India*. ACC Publishing, Woodbridge, UK, 1996.

Ringsrud, Ronald. *Emeralds: a passionate guide*. GVP Publishing, Godyear, Oxnard, California, 2009.

Robinson, Francis. *The Mughal Emperors and the Islamic Dynasties of India, Iran and Central Asia, 1206–1925*. Thames & Hudson, London, 2007.

Roger Keverne, ed. *Jade*. Anness Publishing, London, 1991.

Rousselet, Louis. *India and its Native Princes: travels in central India and in the Presidencies of Bombay and Bengal*, ed. Lieut. Col. Buckle. Bickers and Son, London, 1878.

Saryu, Doshi, Dr, ed. *Pageant of Indian Art: Festival of India in Great Britain*. Marg Publications, Bombay, 1993.

Schumann, Walter. *Elsevier Gids van Edel—en Sierstenen*. Elsevier Focus, Amsterdam, 1985.

Self, J., J. Hardy, F. Sozanni and H. Judah. *Twenty One Centuries of Jewelled Opulence and Power*. Thames & Hudson, London, 2014.

Sharma, Rita Devi and Varadarajan, M. *Handcrafted Indian Enamel Jewellery.* Lustre Press/Roli Books, New Delhi, 2004.

Singh, Daram Vir. *Hinduism: an introduction.* Rupa Publications, New Delhi, 2003.

Spink, M. *A Journey through India: Company School pictures.* Spink, London, 1996. Exhibition catalogue.

Spink, M. *A Journey through India: pictures of India by British artists.* Spink, London, 1996.

Spink, M. *Indian & Islamic Works of Art.* Spink, London, 1992. Exhibition catalogue.

Spink, M., ed. *Islamic and Hindu Jewellery.* Spink, London, 1988. Exhibition catalogue.

Spink, M., ed. *Islamic Jewellery.* Spink, London, 1986. Exhibition catalogue.

Spink, M. *Islamic Jewellery.* Spink, London, 1996. Exhibition catalogue.

Spink, M. *Passion and Tranquility.* Spink, London, 1998. Exhibition catalogue.

Spink, M. *Tibetan Art at Spink.* Spink, London, 1992. Exhibition catalogue.

Spink, M. *Treasures of the Courts.* Spink, London, 1994. Exhibition catalogue.

Srivastava, Sanjeev P. *Jahangir: a connoisseur of Mughal art.* Abhinav Publications, Maharastra, India, 2001.

Streeter, Edwin W. *The Great Diamonds of the World: their history and romance.* G. Bell & Sons, London, 1882.

Stronge, Susan. *Bejewelled Treasures: the Al Thani Collection.* V&A Publishing, London, 2015.

Stronge, Susan. *Painting for the Mughal Emperor: the art of the book 1560-1660.* V&A Publishing, London, 2002.

Stronge, Susan, ed. *The Arts of the Sikh Kingdom.* V&A Publishing, London, 1999.

Stronge, Susan, ed. *The Jewels of India.* Marg Publications, Bombay, 1995.

Stronge, S., N. Smith and J. C. Harle. *A Golden Treasury: jewellery from the Indian subcontinent.* Rizolli, London, 2008.

Swami, Sivapriyananda. *Astrology and Religion in Indian Art.* Abhinav Publications, Cleveland, 1990.

Tank, Raj Roop. *Indian Gemmology.* Dulichand Kirtichand Tank, Jaipur, 1971.

Tavernier, Jean Baptiste. *Travels in India*, trans. V. Ball. Macmillan, London, 1889.

Thackston, Wheeler M. *The Baburnama: memoirs of Babur, prince and emperor*, trans. ed. annot. Wheeler M. Thackston. Oxford University Press, Oxford, 1996.

Thackston, Wheeler. M. *The Jahangirnama: memoirs of Jahangir, Emperor of India*, trans. ed. annot. Wheeler M. Thackston. Oxford Unirversity Press, New York, 1999.

Tod, James. *Annals and Antiquities of Rajasthan: or the central and western Rajput States of India*, 2nd edition, ed. William Crooke. Motilal Banarsidass, New Delhi, India, 1998.

Untracht, Oppi. *Jewelry Concepts and Technology.* Thames & Hudson, London, 1982.

Untracht, Oppi. *Traditional Jewelry of India.* Thames & Hudson, London, 1997.

Van Campen, Jan and Ebeltje Hartkamp-Jonxis. *Asian Splendour: Company art in the Rijksmuseum.* Rijksmuseum, Amsterdam, 2011.

Van Cutsem, Anne. *A World of Earrings.* Skira Editore, Milano, 2001.

Van Cutsem, Anne. *A World of Head Ornaments.* Skira Editore, Milano, 2005.

Van Gelder, Noelle. *The Origin of Quality.* Van Gelder Indian Jewellery, the Netherlands, 2016. Exhibition catalogue.

Vaughn, Howard (part 2). *A Kaleidoscope of Colours: Indian Mughal jewels from the 18th and 19th centuries.* Antwerp Diamond Museum, Antwerp, 1997. Exhibition catalogue.

Von Leyden, Rudolf. *Ganjifa: the playing cards of India.* Victoria and Albert Museum, London, 1982.

Von Leyden, Rudolf. *Indische Spielkarten. Inventarkatalog der Indischen Sammlung des Deutschen Spielkarten-Museums.* Leinfelden-Echterdingen, Germany, 1977.

Vyas, Shimul Mehta. *When Jewellery Speaks.* National Institute of Design, Ahmedabad, India, 2012.

Webster, Robert, ed. *Gems: their sources, descriptions and identification.* Butterworth, UK, 1975.

Weihreter, Hans. *Blumen des Paradieses Der Furstenschmuck Nordindiens.* Graz, Austria, 1997.

Weihreter, Hans. *Schatze der Menschen und Gotter Augsburg.* Khyun, Ausburg, 1993.

Weihreter, Hans. *Schmuck der Maharajas.* Deutscher Kunstverlag, Augsburg, 2012.

Weihreter, Hans. *Schutzende Pracht Indischer Schmuck aus Drei Jahrhunderten.* Edition Khyun, Augsburg, 2008.

Welsh, Stuart Cary. *India, Art and Culture 1300–1900.* MetPublications, New York, 1985.

Williams, George M. *Handbook of Hindu Mythology.* Oxford University Press, Oxford, 2003.

Zebrowski, M. *Gold, Silver & Bronze from Mughal India.* Laurence King, London, 1997.

Zimmer, Heinrich. *Myths and Symbols in Indian Art and Civilization*, ed. Joseph Campbell. Bollingen Series VI, Princeton University Press, Princeton, 1974.

Zucker, Benjamin. *Gems and Jewels: a connoisseur's guide.* Overlook Books, London, 1984.

Index

Vernacular terms are in *italic*
Page numbers in **bold** refer to images

About the Author

Bernadette van Gelder was born into a large well-known merchant family in the south of the Netherlands. After a successful career in the family business she felt it was time for a change.

Being presented with an early nineteenth-century demi parure of traditional Chinese export jewellery encouraged her to study the history behind it; she felt instinctively that this was the path she should take. From China, the road led to India on a quest for magnificent pieces of traditional Indian jewellery.

In the course of this journey she has built a network of business partners, connoisseurs, scholars and, most importantly, friends who have allowed her to access and study royal collections and exquisite pieces of jewellery and works of art.

Thirty-five years of extended field research have established Mrs van Gelder as an internationally renowned expert on traditional Indian jewellery.

For twenty-five years Bernadette van Gelder has been a member of the vetting committee for Indian jewellery at the European Fine Art Fair Maastricht TEFAF, collaborating with Oppi Untracht and PAN Amsterdam.

She curated the exhibition 'Babur's Heritage. The Influence of Mughal Jewellery' at the renowned Diamond Museum, Antwerp in 2006, and curated a loan exhibition entitled 'Traditional Indian Jewellery' during TEFAF Basel 1996.

In 1993, Bernadette was Guest Lecturer at SOAS University of London (the only Higher Education institution in Europe specialising in the study of Asia, Africa and the Near and Middle East).

She has written several catalogues:
2012   'The impulse to adorn: beauty, power & grace'
2011   'Golden treasures of traditional Indian jewellery'
2010   'Moments of beauty'

Bernadette van Gelder is an occasional speaker.

Image Credits

The author and publisher would like to thank the museums, galleries and private collectors who have kindly supplied photographs and/or have allowed us to use their work for reproduction.

In particular we would like to thank:

Mahaveer Swami, Bikaner, India
Miniatures: pages 13, 42, 204

Simon Ray Indian & Islamic Works of Art, London, UK
Miniature: page 233
Emerald necklace: page 234
A Nautch Girl with a Hookah: page 38

Georgia Chrischilles, Brussels, Belgium
Gold *vanki*, *bazuband*, with *nali*, gold ring: pages 18–21

The British Museum, London, UK
Ivory statue: pages 44–45

National Museum of Natural History, National Gem Collection, Smithsonian, Washington, DC, USA
The Rosser Reeves Ruby: page 93
The Hope Diamond: page 171
The Logan Blue: page 226
The Star of Asia: page 227
The Star of Bombay: page 227

Christies, London, UK
The Blue Giant of the Orient: page 226

Spink & Son, London, UK
A Nautch Girl with a Hookah: page 38

The Museum of Islamic Art, Doha, Qatar
Emperor Akbar's Pearl: page 128
The Mogul Mughal: page 235

The State Hermitage, St Petersburg, Russia
Portrait of Zinaida Yusupova: page 133

Natural History Museum, London, UK
The Hope Pearl: page 132

Royal Collection Trust, London, UK
The Koh-i-nûr armlet: page 167
The Black Prince's Ruby: page 253

Victoria and Albert Museum, London, UK
Carew Spinel: page 254

The Field Museum, Chicago, USA
Nur Jahan Spinel, page 255

Mr and Mrs Mis, Brussels, Belgium
Front and back cover images, pages 270–277

All other photographs are author's own.

ISBN 978 1 85149 883 3

Page 1: Gold image of Lord Ganesha, see pages 16–17

Frontispiece: Gold *bazuband*, see pages 172–173

Title page: Gold *tikka*, see pages 180–181

Endpapers: Map of Rajasthan by Mahaveer Swami, Bikaner, India

Front and back covers: Jewelled pendant in the style of a single flower, and its polychrome enamelled
reverse, see pages 270–277. Courtesy of Mr and Mrs Mis, Brussels, Belgium

Printed in Belgium
for ACC Art Books Ltd, Woodbridge, Suffolk, IP12 4SD, UK
www.accartbooks.com

राजस्थान